British History in Perspective
General Editor: Jeremy Black

PUBLISHED TITLES

Rodney Barker *Politics, Peoples and Government*
C. J. Bartlett *British Foreign Policy in the Twentieth Century*
Jeremy Black *Robert Walpole and the Nature of Politics
in Early Eighteenth-Century Britain*
Anne Curry *The Hundred Years War*
John W. Derry *British Politics in the Age of Fox, Pitt and Liverpool*
William Gibson *Church, State and Society, 1760–1850*
Brian Golding *Conquest and Colonisation: the Normans
in Britain, 1066–1100*
Steven Gunn *Early Tudor Government, 1485–1558*
Richard Harding *The Evolution of the Sailing Navy, 1509–1815*
Ann Hughes *The Causes of the English Civil War*
Ronald Hutton *The British Republic, 1649–1660*
Kevin Jefferys *The Labour Party since 1945*
D. M. Loades *The Mid-Tudor Crisis, 1545–1565*
Diarmaid MacCulloch *The Later Reformation in England, 1547–1603*
W. M. Ormrod *Political Life in Medieval England, 1300–1450*
Keith Perry *British Politics and the American Revolution*
A. J. Pollard *The Wars of the Roses*
David Powell *British Politics and the Labour Question, 1868–1990*
Michael Prestwich *English Politics in the Thirteenth Century*
Richard Rex *Henry VIII and the English Reformation*
G. R. Searle *The Liberal Party: Triumph and Disintegration, 1886–1929*
Paul Seaward *The Restoration, 1660–1668*
Robert Stewart *Party and Politics, 1830–1852*
John W. Young *Britain and European Unity, 1945–92*

History of Ireland

D. G. Boyce *The Irish Question and British Politics, 1868–1986*
David Harkness *Ireland in the Twentieth Century: Divided Island*

History of Scotland

Keith M. Brown *Kingdom or Province? Scotland and the Regal Union,
1603–1715*

History of Wales

A. D. Carr *Medieval Wales*
J. Gwynfor Jones *Early Modern Wales, c.1525–1640*

Please see overleaf for forthcoming titles

FORTHCOMING TITLES

Walter L. Arnstein *Queen Victoria*
Eugenio Biagini *Gladstone*
Peter Catterall *The Labour Party, 1918–1940*
Gregory Claeys *The French Revolution Debate in Britain*
Pauline Croft *James I*
Eveline Cruickshanks *The Glorious Revolution*
John Davis *British Politics, 1885–1939*
David Dean *Parliament and Politics in Elizabethan and Jacobean England, 1558–1614*
Susan Doran *English Foreign Policy in the Sixteenth Century*
David Eastwood *Government and Community in the Provinces: England, 1750–1850*
Colin Eldridge *The Victorians Overseas*
Richard English *The IRA*
Angus Hawkins *British Party Politics, 1852–1886*
T. A. Jenkins *Disraeli*
H. S. Jones *Political Thought in Nineteenth-Century Britain*
D. E. Kennedy *The English Revolution, 1642–1649*
Anthony Milton *Church and Religion in England, 1603–1642*
R. C. Nash *English Foreign Trade and the World Economy, 1600–1800*
Richard Ovendale *Anglo-American Relations in the Twentieth Century*
Ian Parker *Lloyd George*
David Powell *The Edwardian Crisis: Britain, 1901–1914*
Robin Prior and Trevor Wilson *Britain and the Impact of World War I*
Brian Quintrell *Government and Politics in Early Stuart England*
Stephen Roberts *Governance in England and Wales, 1603–1688*
W. Stafford *John Stuart Mill*
Alan Sykes *The Radical Right in Britain*
Ann Williams *Kingship and Government in Pre-Conquest England*
Michael Young *Charles I*

History of Ireland

Toby Barnard *The Kingdom of Ireland, 1641–1740*
Sean Duffy *Ireland in the Middle Ages*
Alan Heesom *The Anglo-Irish Union, 1800–1922*
Hiram Morgan *Ireland in the Early Modern Periphery, 1534–1690*

History of Scotland

I. G. C. Hutchinson *Scottish Politics in the Twentieth Century*
Roger Mason *Kingship and Tyranny? Scotland, 1513–1603*
John McCaffrey *Scotland in the Nineteenth Century*
John Shaw *The Political History of Eighteenth-Century Scotland*
Bruce Webster *Scotland in the Middle Ages*

History of Wales

Gareth Jones *Wales, 1700–1980: Crises of Identity*

IRELAND IN THE TWENTIETH CENTURY

DIVIDED ISLAND

DAVID HARKNESS

St. Martin's Press   New York

St. Martin's Press, Scholarly and Reference Division,
175 Fifth Avenue, New York, N.Y. 10010

First published in the United States of America in 1996

Printed in Malaysia

ISBN 0–312–12663–8

Library of Congress Cataloging-in-Publication Data
Harkness, David
Ireland in the twentieth century:divided island / David
Harkness.
p.   cm. — (British history in perspective)
Includes bibliographical references (p.   ) and index .
ISBN 0–312–12663–8
1. Ireland—Politics and government—20th century.   2. Northern
Ireland—Politics and government—1969–   3. Nationalism—Ireland–
–History—20th century.   4. Irish unification question.   I. Title.
II. Series.
DA959.H37   1995
320.5'4'09415—dc20   95–9736
                                                              CIP

CONTENTS

Preface   viii

Acknowledgements   x

1 Home Rule and Unionism: to 1912   1

2 No Compromise: 1913–18   20

3 Division and Retrenchment: 1919–25   34

4 Separate Ways: 1926–38   47

5 Neutral and Belligerent: 1938–49   64

6 Neighbours of a Kind: 1950–72   84

7 London Steps In: 1972–92   100

8 Conclusion   115

Appendix A Extracts from the Government of Ireland
                Act, 1920   127

Appendix B Articles of Agreement for a Treaty
                between Great Britain and Ireland, 1921   137

Contents

Appendix C   Ireland (Confirmation of Agreement)
                 Act, 1925   144

Appendix D   Extracts from the Irish Constitutions of
                 1922 and 1937   148

Appendix E   The Republic of Ireland Act, 1948, and
                 the Ireland Act, 1949   159

Appendix F   The Anglo-Irish Agreement,
                 15 November 1985   167

Notes   177

Index   185

To the memory of
Rita Alice Harkness

PREFACE

There are several histories of Ireland in the twentieth century. This is not one of them. Rather, it recounts the relationship between the Irish nationalist community in the larger part of the island and the unionist community in its north-eastern corner. They held diametrically opposite views on the desirability of the maintenance of the United Kingdom of Great Britain and Ireland as a single entity as the twentieth century opened and they have adhered to their views since: through an independence movement that reached its peak after the First World War and succeeded in detaching 26 of Ireland's 32 counties from subjection to Westminster; through an interwar period of depression and economic decline; through a Second World War which greatly enhanced the barrier between them; and since, through fifty years of fluctuating fortunes, a further campaign of violence and the replacement of devolved local government in Belfast by direct rule from London.

This account traces the incompatibilities of the two allegiances over more than ninety years. It picks out the many areas of difference and the occasional high-profile points of agreement and co-operation. What is not well documented but which should not be ignored is the constant low level contact and co-operation between individuals, groups and institutions on a day-to-day basis at virtually all times in this period, even during the past twenty-five years of paramilitary violence in Northern Ireland. Families have crossed and re-crossed a border which has grown progressively less meaningful as joint membership of the European Community has developed. Churches, a range of professional and educational bodies, and some major sporting organisations have always maintained all-Ireland structures. Railways and bus lines have continued to operate across the frontier. Commercial, cultural and social co-operation has been preserved at many levels, and tourism has attracted citizens of each to the other. Despite the self-preoccupation and the differences of opinion which the pages that follow enumerate, at ground level those who inhabit the island have managed to get on well enough together. That basic reality is fundamental. It has kept even the worst of times from the destructive scale of civil conflicts in other parts of the world. It is the best reason for hoping that it is yet possible that arrangements can be made for all who live on the island to do so in peace and mutual respect.

Concern for human rights, commitment to democratic values and an acceptance that many views of the past are legitimate can combine to help the process of living together. Awareness can lead to understanding. Understanding can facilitate tolerance. It is in optimistic trust in these truths that this book has been written.

ACKNOWLEDGEMENTS

Extracts from the Irish Free State Constitution (1922), the Constitution of Ireland (1937) and the Republic of Ireland Act (1948) are all reproduced with permission of the Controller, Stationery Office, Dublin.

Crown copyright is reproduced with the permission of the Controller of HMSO.

1

HOME RULE AND UNIONISM: TO 1912

Ireland entered the twentieth century as part of the United Kingdom of Great Britain and Ireland, the second island, an area of some 32,595 square miles, with a population, according to the 1901 census, of 4,458,775. Joined, on 1 January 1801, to Britain by the Act of Union, Ireland as a whole had not prospered in the nineteenth century, despite being hitched to the world's leading industrial and imperial power. As communications increased, literacy expanded and democratic institutions advanced, the discontents of a largely rural, Catholic people within an urban, Protestant kingdom steadily found their voice.

Catholic Ireland had begun at a disadvantage under the Union, and the fact that three decades had passed before political equality with Protestants was achieved in law had done much to disenchant politically aware Catholics. Besides, Ireland was not governed as the rest of the kingdom: a separate administration persisted in Dublin; legislation remained different; and throughout most of the island an expanding population and a declining economy resulted in greater poverty and more frequent famines. Irish Catholic leaders, blaming the Union for their condition, sought to undo it.

For Protestants in Ireland, the perspective was different. A favoured, minority establishment spread thinly over the island, Protestants had surrendered their parliament in 1800 to secure the safety of numbers within an overwhelmingly Protestant United Kingdom. The American and French revolutions had raised the spectre of democracy, where numbers, not privilege or property, would prevail, and a section of the Protestant elite took sufficient fright to accept London's plan for Union. War with France and Irish parliamentary intractability had both roused the anxiety and taxed the patience of the London authorities. Union seemed a better way of managing Anglo-Irish relations, so Union was rushed through, using ruthlessly the powers available in that unreformed parliamentary era.

The Irish Protestant establishment was deeply divided, however, with many opposing the Union plan. Protestants dominated Ireland and were particularly strong in the north east where seventeenth-century English and Scots plantation and much subsequent settlement had produced Protestant majorities in several counties. They did not trust Westminster to manage Irish affairs in their interest as well as they could manage it themselves. Dismissing the prospects of democracy, they preferred to remain masters in their own house.

The early nineteenth-century experience, that had disillusioned Catholics, served to win the bulk of Protestants to the Union, however, for their monopoly of power continued, they controlled political representation, their landed power was upheld, and their minority church remained established. In the north-east alone industrial development occurred, linking Belfast, a fast growing Victorian city, into the industrial and trading nexus of the Clyde and the Mersey. Protestant political, religious and economic interests became indissolubly associated with the Union. And to these interests were added a cultural dimension as Catholic discontent, given initial focus by specifically Catholic disabilities, embraced ideas of romantic nationalism which sought validity in Gaelic language and traditions distinct from the British heritage of the oppressive neighbouring island and of their Protestant fellow citizens.

The scene was set for strife. Daniel O'Connell, having secured Catholic political emancipation in 1829, and having spent the 1830s giving the reformed Westminster parliament an opportunity to confer equal justice upon Ireland, finally despaired of that possibility and demanded the return of an Irish parliament to manage Irish affairs. His Repeal movement was unsuccessful. Significantly, his 1841 attempt to convince the north was rejected. Already industrial development had gone too far. The arguments for Union had been raised all around in factories, in urban dwellings, civic buildings and in bustling intellectual activity. 'Look at Belfast', the Protestant champion Henry Cooke cried, 'and be a Repealer – if you can'.[1]

The booming activity of the north-east, its contrasting character and its dynamic energy were visible for all to see as the century advanced. In 1864, France, long accustomed to placing commercial representatives in major ports around the world, recognised reality by sending a professional diplomat to Belfast to add to its consul in Dublin, a post occupied since 1815. In the 1880s Irish division came to a head when the expansion of the franchise, specific hardship on the land, and a capable nationalist leadership coincided to mount a formidable assault on the status quo. Parnell's Home Rule movement, demanding Irish management of Irish affairs through an Irish parliament in Dublin, backed by widespread electoral success and following the disestablishment of the Church of Ireland in 1869, and the steady erosion of Protestant landed, central and local government power, forced the leadership of that privileged minority to organise resistance.

They did so effectively. Mobilised in the south, west and east to harness landed wealth, in the north to generate a popular outcry, and in the shires of England calling up resources of kin and of kindred feeling, the supporters of Union mounted their defence. In 1886 in the House of Commons, and in 1893 in the Lords, two Home Rule Bills put forward by Liberal governments were defeated. The Conservative and Unionist Party regained ascendancy and the Union was saved.

But for how long? The Irish Home Rule movement split and diminished itself in the aftermath of the Parnell divorce scandal in 1890. It endured a decade of weakness before combining once more in 1900 under the leadership of John Redmond. By this year electoral demand had been expressed clearly in Ireland at four successive elections and was about to be expressed at a fifth: three-quarters of the constituencies had returned Home Rulers of one sort or another; and this had been backed by further success in the first Irish local government elections in 1898. But the Tory government, pursuing a strategy of removing nationalist grievances, had enjoyed some success too, and still hoped that Home Rule could be 'killed by kindness'. As it made more and more concessions to nationalist opinion, however, approving the appointment of nationalists to administrative posts, conciliating Catholic educational interests, reforming local government to give free play to democracy, and even, it seemed in 1904, toying with plans for devolving some governmental authority to Dublin, so the dismay of its Unionist allies in Ireland grew apace. Once more alarm bells sounded in Belfast. In March 1905 Unionists in the north formed an Ulster Unionist Council, a standing organisation to keep watch on events and to call to concerted action if need be the range of political and religious bodies that gave meaning to Unionism in the province. Home Rule, dubbed 'Rome Rule' in the 1880s, must be prevented at all costs.

There is nothing intrinsically significant about the first year of a new century, but it is inevitably a time when people and organisations take stock. During a war against the Boer republics, with a Conservative and Unionist government in power, and with their own adversaries divided, there was no great cause for Unionist worry as the twentieth century dawned, even though, as noted, things had grown worse by 1905. For nationalists, in January 1900 matters were in flux. The centenary, two years earlier, of the 1798 rebellion had in one sense exposed much cause for shame: no progress with home rule; an ineffective political party; the risk that better government might satisfy the people and reduce their demand for self-government; and by 1900 the contrast between a passive Ireland and the determined belligerents of the Orange Free State and the Transvaal seemed stark. At the same time much had been achieved in the 1880s and 1890s to renew interest in those features of Ireland's past that lent it distinctiveness. The Gaelic Athletic Association, founded in

4

1884, had done much to revive and codify native sports; the Gaelic League, 1893, to rejuvenate interest in a language almost extinguished by the twin ravages of the Great Famine and an educational system conducted in English. There had been a resurgence in the writing of history, the recovery of folk tales and tradition, and a new energy in literary and theatrical creativity. The Roman Catholic religion had enjoyed a renewal in church building, a centralising revolution and new uniformity of practice. While there had been notable Protestant contribution to scholarly and literary achievement, the general thrust was to give new pride and confidence to Irish nationality.

John Redmond, when he became the leader of the reunited Irish Parliamentary Party on 6 February 1900, claimed to stand where Parnell had stood, and to uphold the tradition of Irish nationality that stretched back beyond Thomas Davis in the 1840s and Wolfe Tone in the 1790s: a wide-ranging nationality that was inclusive, embracing those of all creeds and backgrounds.

It is true that Redmond was a Home Ruler, that he sought Ireland's liberty within the structure of a United Kingdom and a British Empire which he felt gave Irishmen great opportunities, to which, after all, they were entitled, given the contribution they had made to imperial development. It is true also that there were others around him who had more radical and independent aims, but there was no disagreement between mild devolutionists at one end of the spectrum and absolute separatists at the other that they were both concerned with the whole island of Ireland and with a single nation within it. As Redmond was to state later when confronted by Unionist denials of this claim, to argue that there were two nations in Ireland 'was an abomination and a blasphemy'.[2]

In 1900 it was not yet clear that this was the issue at stake. There were, within the nationalist camp, republicans who stood four square for the complete severance of Ireland from Britain advocated by Tone; followers of Arthur Griffith, soon to develop a Dual Monarchy, Sinn Fein alternative, with an independent Irish parliament sharing with Britain a common sovereign; and Home Rulers seeking devolution from Westminster to a Dublin parliament of the powers to manage specifically Irish affairs, while retaining representation at Westminster for matters of wider British and imperial concern. They might not all have recognised one another as bedfellows.

Arranged against the separatists were the upholders of the existing state. It may have been the case that the Liberal Party was still committed to Home Rule, but its members adhered to the belief that this measure would serve, by making the Irish more contented, to strengthen the state; and some even believed that more devolution should follow in other regions, leading to a federal kingdom. A necessary condition for success in Ireland, it was felt, was the harnessing of the resources of the United Kingdom to a resolution of the land problem. But these views, and to a greater extent those of the Irish nationalists, were adamantly opposed by the ruling Conservative and Unionist Party, which derided Liberal folly, distrusted Irish intentions and dismissed Irish capacities, fearing the break-up of the state and the dissolution of the Empire, which alone could keep Britain 'Great' in the years ahead. Within Ireland the bulk of the Protestant community opposed any concession to nationalist sentiment. Protestants may have regarded themselves as Irish but underlying this was a commitment to the values associated with the British state: liberal, individualistic, just – and Protestant.

During the first two decades of the new century, while other great issues of national and international importance were being shaped, these allegiances clashed in Ireland, clarified and simplified. The constitutional struggle between Lords and Commons provided the catalyst, the third Home Rule Bill the occasion, while bitter inter-party rivalry, allied to extremities of intransigence and the impact of a deteriorating European order, imposed unexpected distortions on the outcome. Ireland's twentieth-century development followed no inevitable or straightforward path.

With the victory of the Conservative government in the 'khaki' election of October 1900, Redmond's Nationalist Party could only continue to work as best it could with an essentially hostile regime. The Conservatives offered a programme of conciliation calculated to remove those grievances which, in its own view, constituted nationalism. Like the Liberals, they adopted a policy of land reform which, from the mid 1880s, had in practice involved the search for a formula by which tenants could purchase their holdings, and landlords, ideally, could remain in place, well compensated for what they sold, well set to continue to farm their home demesnes if they so wished. Conservatives hoped, and Nationalists feared, that success would reconcile the bulk of Irishmen to the Union, that the natural order of society would be preserved and that a numerous and conservative peasant proprietary would be established, prosperous and secure, and grateful to the state and the party that had so endowed it.

In 1903, the Wyndham Land Act embodied the long-sought-for formula and the great transfer of land took off. Unluckily for many of the purchasers and for the enthusiasts of prosperity and gratitude, a large number of the transferred holdings proved hopelessly uneconomic. Problems and poverty remained and the process in any case took time. Irish management of Irish affairs, therefore, continued to be a goal, and not only in the form of Home Rule.

More extreme ambitions had long been voiced. The Irish Republican Brotherhood (IRB), the inheritor of the Fenian movement, had passed through a moribund stage but soon after the start of the century its membership began to show signs of new vigour. Committed to the winning of an independent republic by force of arms, it had as yet neither the organisation nor the opportunity for dramatic action. But it was newly determined to acquire both.

Also in the shadows as yet were the schemes and activities of Arthur Griffith. A twenty-nine-year-old journalist in 1900, Griffith had spent a couple of years in South Africa before returning to Dublin in 1898, to edit the weekly *United Irishman*. Particularly interested in the political history of Hungary and the economic history of Germany, Griffith hammered out in the opening years of the century a plan for the achievement of

Irish self-government and a programme of economic renewal, using opportunities as they arose to form societies and disseminate his views. In 1903, for example, he founded the National Council to protest against the visit of Edward VII to Ireland. He encouraged the amalgamation of other activist clubs, in 1907, under the umbrella of his latest creation, the Sinn Fein League (after 1908 simply Sinn Fein). Griffith advocated the withdrawal of Irish Representatives from Westminster, where they were always outnumbered by the representatives of non-Irish areas, and the establishment by them of an Irish Assembly. His model was Hungary and he was prepared to carry the model further and accept King Edward as a Dual Monarch along Austro-Hungarian lines. His economic policy followed the example of Frederick List and sought to develop Ireland's resources to a much greater degree of self-sufficiency. He was successful in spreading his ideas, but only thinly and on a small scale as yet, for the return to government of the Liberals and their victory in the polls in 1906 gave a new boost to the fortunes of the followers of Redmond. The Home Rulers, with their allies in power, must surely achieve a measure of self-government for Ireland. They must be encouraged to achieve as much as possible. In the meantime, the separatists would wait and watch.

In viewing their many ambitions and policies, the new Liberal government, led by Sir Henry Campbell-Bannerman, included a promise to advance Irish Home Rule, but this matter was not so urgent as issues of social and economic policy and would be implemented only gradually, along with other Irish reforms, as time and occasion permitted. A parliamentary majority of 84 over all other parties meant that the Liberals did not have to rely on Redmond's support, so, although the situation was now much more favourable to the Irish Party, it could exert no leverage to accelerate its goal.

Even so, relations between Redmond and Campbell-Bannerman were good, the case so long argued for Home Rule was accepted, and minor palliatives in 1906 were followed by what was intended to be a first instalment of devolution in 1907. Campbell-Bannerman himself referred to his Irish Council Bill as 'a little, modest, shy, humble effort to give administrative powers to the Irish people'.[3] It proposed a Council of 106, to administer 8 out of the 45 existing Dublin departments. They were the most important, however, and accounted for over half of the Administration. In the event, Irish public opinion derided the scheme when it appeared and at a National Convention on 21 May Redmond, who might have been willing to give it a try, was forced to denounce it. It was immediately withdrawn.

In the space of three years, therefore, Conservatives had sought to conciliate the Irish by suggesting some devolved responsibility, only to be pulled back by Unionists outraged at their going too far; and Liberals, endeavouring to encourage their Irish allies by a partial measure, had been repulsed by those very allies complaining that they were not going far enough. The Irish question did not offer easy resolution.

Cordial relations persisted between Redmond and the Prime Minister, however, and consultation proceeded as before. A major landmark was reached on 1 August 1908 when third-level education in Ireland was transformed by an Irish Universities Act which did much to satisfy Catholic aspirations in this area by establishing two universities from the old Royal University structure. The first was a federal National University of Ireland, combining the University Colleges of Cork, Galway and Dublin; the second transformed the remaining University College into the Queen's University of Belfast, and 'by a curious freak of timing, anticipated by a few years in the sphere of education the coming political division of the country into north and south'.[4] By the time of its enactment, however, Campbell-Bannerman had died and been replaced in office by H. H. Asquith, a somewhat less enthusiastic Home Ruler.

Asquith did oversee the amendment of the Wyndham Act's depleted finances in 1909 before being plunged by his Chancellor, Lloyd George, into head-on conflict with the Tory-dominated House of Lords. The ensuing constitutional crisis, the general elections necessary before its resolution, and the consequent transformation of the Lords' veto into a mere delaying power, were to commit Asquith firmly to his Irish allies and to give Redmond the opportunity to gain real Home Rule: no 'modest' half measure but a full devolution of self-government along Gladstonian lines.

The dramatic story of the struggle for supremacy between the elected and the hereditary Chambers is peripheral to this narrative but its outcome is absolutely central. The Conservative House of Lords, irritated at loss of government office, distrustful of Liberal economic and social interventionism, and finally goaded by clever tax proposals which threatened landed property, added to their record of dismissing Liberal bills by rejecting the Budget on 30 November 1909. Asquith went to the country, not on the Budget but on the issue of the Lords' power of veto.

On the eve of the January 1910 election, with the votes of the Irish in England at least partly in mind, the Prime Minister made a Home Rule promise: 'a system of full self-government in regard to purely Irish affairs'.[5] The electorate responded with almost even-handed backing for the two major parties: 275 Liberals were returned, and 273 Conservatives. Labour, no friend of the Lords, gained 40 seats, the Irish 82. Asquith did not need Irish support to govern, but he could not afford Irish opposition. A Home Rule Bill must follow, but how, first, could the Upper Chamber be put in its place?

Any bill trimming the Lords' power required the acceptance of a Lords' majority. Either the existing Lords must accept the will of the electorate and act accordingly, or the King would have to create enough new Liberal peers to ensure such action, something he was prepared to do only after a second election confirming the electorate's approval of the proposed measure. Curbing legislation (the Parliament Bill) was passed by the Commons on 25 April. Then, on 6 May, Edward died. The Lords had not yet considered the bill. But should a young and inexperienced George V be faced at the beginning of his reign with such contentious decisions?

From June until November, in private sessions of a constitutional conference, eight Liberal and Conservative leaders sought a compromise, until on 10 November their talks finally broke down. They failed because the Conservative leader, Balfour, refused in the end to imperil, as he saw it, either the unity of the kingdom or the unity of the Conservative Party. But the very fact of these talks altered the situation. The compromises discussed included areas of significance: the recognition of Commons authority in all but such vital matters as the Union; the rather more distant prospect of federation, or devolution-all-round; and even a coalition to surmount the party-political impasse.

Throughout these months, the Irish were on tenterhooks, excluded and kept in the dark, not knowing if their prize would elude them; Unionists in Ireland were better informed but almost equally alarmed at looming bipartisan agreements that seemed to go too far for their liking. Breakdown relieved the Irish Home Rulers and cemented the alliance of Conservatives and Irish Unionists, who could stand together on the Union whatever else transpired.

Asquith now put the Parliament Bill to the Lords, where it was quickly rejected, and a second general election followed in December. The terms of the Parliament Bill were put before the people, and the people returned their representatives in almost exactly the same terms as in January.

The 1911 Parliament Act, passed in dramatic circumstances by the Lords without the need for Liberal augmentation, on 10 August 1911, effectively reduced the Lords' veto power to a capacity to delay legislation for two years; the time it would take a rejected bill to complete the required further two circuits of parliamentary procedures. Once the Parliament Act had been made law, the way was open for a third Home Rule Bill that would not be subject to rejection but would most probably be held up to the limit. Such a bill was introduced by Asquith on 11 April 1912. It was a measure of very modest dimensions, in some ways a retreat even from the cautious bills of 1886 and 1893, but even before its introduction to parliament it had occasioned violent turmoil in Ireland, and during its hotly disputed passage it gave rise to a vehemence of language and action seldom associated with constitutionalism. Why should so restricted a devolution bill have become the centre of such passion?

The answer lies in the incompatible aspirations of Nationalists and Unionists and their fundamentally opposed perceptions of the Bill's longer-term implications. Within the spectrum of Irish Nationalism there had been periodic differences as to the method of achieving the goal, and the goal itself had traditionally stretched well beyond the mere restoration of parliamentary institutions of limited, local authority, but all nationalists shared assumptions that were to them self-evident, long-standing and incontrovertible: that the Irish nation was ancient, that it embraced the whole island and all who lived within it, and that it cherished the contribution and well-being of all.

Full-blown republicans assuredly sought independence by force of arms. The Irish Republican Brotherhood, whose Supreme Council regarded itself also as the 'Government of the Irish Republic', had long declared the 'inherent and inalienable' right of Ireland 'to self-government and independent nationhood', and had spoken of a 'hatred of English rule . . . confined to no rank, no creed, no province of Ireland' which pervaded 'the conscience of the whole people inherent and undying'. The Council had 'sought to place the Irish Republic in a respectable and dignified position' – a position demanded by Robert Emmet at his trial in 1803, and one vividly recalled on the centenary of his death, in well orchestrated commemoration, in 1903 – and its very Constitution recorded that 'the Irish people have never ceased to struggle for the recovery of their independence since the date of its destruction'.[6]

And the IRB, dormant as an elderly leadership lived out its time, reduced in numbers and insignificant in impact, was transformed in quality and revitalised by younger, less patient men in these first years of the twentieth century: young men like Dennis McCullough, Bulmer Hobson, Sean MacDermott, and Patrick McCartan and P. S. O'Hegarty; and one 'old man in a hurry', Tom Clarke, who had endured imprisonment for Fenian activity, had spent a decade in America and who now returned to Ireland in 1907. These were the activists who breathed new life into the 'Organisation', starting a youth movement and a newspaper and gaining dominance in the Supreme Council between 1908 and 1914. They infiltrated cultural and sporting bodies, initiated political clubs (Dungannon Clubs, for example, begun in 1905 by Hobson and McCullough) or joined existing parties, Griffith's Sinn Fein in particular.

Griffith himself, developing his ideas and organisations in these years, sought a peaceful rather than a violent separation from British interference. It was the controlling hand of Westminster he wished to remove, so that Ireland's own genius could flourish according to its own lights, in Ireland: all of Ireland. Politically, culturally and socially Ireland was one: and economically the whole of Ireland's resources were essential if a balanced and self-sufficient economy was to be built. Best translated as 'We Ourselves', Sinn Fein was unequivocally committed to the 'We' comprehending all of Ireland's people.

But it was Home Rulers who were in the ascendant now, and it was Redmond who had to explain to his opponents in Westminster his vision of nationhood. And Redmond had no doubt at all that Thomas Davis had rightly called all to respond to

a Nationality which will not only raise our people from their poverty, by securing them the blessings of a DOMESTIC LEGISLATURE, but inflame and purify them with a lofty and heroic love of country – a Nationality of the spirit as well as the letter. . . which may embrace Protestant, Catholic and Dissenter – Milesian and Cromwellian – the Irishman of a hundred generations and the stranger who is within our gates. . .[7]

and was right also to direct the energies of his compatriots to

the country of our birth, our education of our recollections, ancestral, personal, national: the country of our loves, our friendships, our hopes, our country.[8]

The facts, after all, spoke for themselves. The latest census, in 1911, simply underlined the situation. Of a total population, now reduced to 4,390,219, the overwhelming majority, some 73.86 per cent, were Roman Catholic. Of the three provinces apart from Ulster, around 250,000 (10 per cent) were Protestant, relatively thinly spread amongst 2,500,000 Roman Catholics. Even in Ulster, where Protestants formed a majority, their 891,000 were faced by 691,000 Roman Catholics, and given the concentration of Protestants in the north-east, there were actually Roman Catholic majorities in five of the nine Ulster counties. Although religion and political allegiance might not always have coincided, they provided a very accurate guide, the one to the other. The second general election of 1910 had returned for Ireland 83 Nationalists and 1 Liberal, against 19 of the Conservative and Unionist Party. In the province of Ulster, on the Home Rule issue, the balance was fine, with 15 Nationalists and 1 Liberal against 17 Unionists. In January 1913 the balance tipped the other way with a Liberal by-election victory in Londonderry City.

For his part, Redmond repeatedly returned to the same theme as the successive Reading and Committee stages of the bill progressed. He put forward Home Rule for Ireland

> as a national demand. . . . The national demand, the national spirit, has been the soul of the movement ever since the Union was carried. We claim that Ireland is a nation, made up, no doubt, by the intermixing of many races. . . . We say that Ireland is a nation. . . a national unit to-day, just as much as England, or Scotland or Wales! . . .We are putting our case forward as a case of a nation and it is on that ground that our claim rests, and from that claim it will never be divorced.[9]

In his eloquent opening speech Asquith had recommended Home Rule, as Gladstone had before him, as the consistent demand of a people at last articulate through democratic institutions, a people that he too had referred to as 'the Irish Nation'. Asquith had also referred to that important and vociferous element of opposition within Ireland but had asserted unequivocally that 'we cannot admit, and we will not admit, the right of a minority of the people, and relatively a small minority . . . to veto the verdict of the vast body of their countrymen'.[10] Redmond had to tackle this issue head on, once an amendment had been tabled in the Committee stage, in June, to exclude four of the most Protestant Ulster counties from the operation of the bill. 'The idea of two nations in Ireland', he averred, 'is to us revolting and hateful. The idea of our agreeing to the partition of our nation is unthinkable. We want the union in Ireland of all creeds, of all classes, of all races, and we would resist most violently as far as it is within our power to do so. . . . To attempt to cut off the Protestants under a two-nation theory from the national traditions and aspirations of the Irish race sounds to many of us something like sacrilege'.[11]

Redmond dismissed the possibility of any other solution than that, as in the past in Canada and South Africa, men of opposing camps should come together and 'govern themselves with mutual toleration',[12] and he assured the Commons that, given Home Rule in Ireland, 'men will come together; they will forget the past; they will sit down at the same table and endeavour to do all they can for the welfare and freedom of their common country'.[13] As to this specific proposal of exclusion,

> we oppose it, because it would destroy for ever our most cherished ambition, namely, to see the Irish nation in the near future made up of every race and every creed and every class working unitedly for the well being and freedom of the Irish race and doing so through the instrumentality of a native Government which, in the words of Thomas Davis
>
> > 'Shall rule by the right and might of all
> > Yet yield to the arrogance of none'.[14]

When, in a final effort to avert catastrophe, a further proposal was made, in January 1913, to exclude the whole of Ulster and thus avoid the coercion of the Northern Protestants under a rule they detested, Redmond again referred to his party's vision and to the lessons of history. 'The Home Rule question is for us the demand of a nation, for the restoration of its national rights.' As to detestable rule, what had the government done in 1800? Then practically all Irishmen, Protestants included, had been placed against their will under such a rule. Would the government now 'coerce the rest of Ireland to continue to live under a system of rule established at the Union which they loathe and have loathed from that day to this?' Redmond rejected any form of division or exclusion: 'Ireland for us is an entity. It is one land.'[15]

To such a view, so often asserted, so seldom demonstrated, Unionists objected. Determined to preserve the United Kingdom, they questioned the validity of using Ireland as a unit at all. Within the total population of the existing state the government was proposing to appease an unappeasable minority in the south and west of Ireland by a measure that would expose the state to disintegration and the Empire to dissolution. In Britain, the members of the Conservative Party, galled by election defeats, outraged by the Parliament Act, riven by disagreements on tariff reform, and to some extent genuinely fearful of the consequences for their Irish allies, were glad to unite to oppose so unnecessary and dangerous a bill.

In Ireland, southern and northern Unionists alike felt their very survival was at stake, but it was in the north that strength lay and it was there that the most comprehensive and vehement campaign was mounted to prevent Home Rule. Demonstrations and declarations followed one another, none more potent or representative than that of 28 September 1912: Ulster Day, the day of the signing of the Covenant. A brilliant propaganda document, couched in religious language and recalling the sixteenth-century Scottish Covenant, it played on genuine misgivings in Ulster but appealed also to the interests of their Conservative allies in Britain. It encapsulated ancient economic, religious and cultural fears that lie at the core of Irish division.

The disaster to Ulster and Ireland's 'material well-being' would inevitably follow the mismanagement of Ireland's affairs by an inexperienced and incompetent regime of Catholic politicians, representing rural constituencies, who would be motivated by greed and blinkered by ideology. They would

Ulster's
Solemn League and Covenant.

Being convinced in our consciences that Home Rule would be disastrous to the material well-being of Ulster as well as of the whole of Ireland, subversive of our civil and religious freedom, destructive of our citizenship and perilous to the unity of the Empire, we, whose names are underwritten, men of Ulster, loyal subjects of His Gracious Majesty King George V., humbly relying on the God whom our fathers in days of stress and trial confidently trusted, do hereby pledge ourselves in solemn Covenant throughout this our time of threatened calamity to stand by one another in defending for ourselves and our children our cherished position of equal citizenship in the United Kingdom and in using all means which may be found necessary to defeat the present conspiracy to set up a Home Rule Parliament in Ireland. ¶ And in the event of such a Parliament being forced upon us we further solemnly and mutually pledge ourselves to refuse to recognise its authority. ¶ In sure confidence that God will defend the right we hereto subscribe our names. ¶ And further, we individually declare that we have not already signed this Covenant.

The above was signed by me at _Belfast._
"Ulster Day," Saturday, 28th September, 1912.

Edward Carson

God Save the King.

The Ulster Solemn League and Covenant, signed by Sir Edward Carson, reproduced by kind permission of HMSO from P. Buckland, (ed.), *Irish Unionism, 1885–1923* (Belfast, 1973) p. 224.[16]

adopt policies of protection, designed to foster development elsewhere in Ireland, which would damage existing industry and end up ruining north and south. The great shipyards of Belfast, the linen industry of the north, its rope works and textile machinery plants, its shirt factories and its tobacco products would all be at hazard. Ulster men and women in the working streets of the province's cities and towns rejected the government's right to hand them over to their enemies. As a proposed preamble to the Covenant put it: 'it is incompetent for any authority, party, or people to appoint as our rulers a Government dominated by men disloyal to the Empire and to whom our faith and traditions are alike hateful.'[17] They would have endorsed Lord Salisbury's observation in Belfast on the eve of Ulster Day: 'The Government of such men (as Mr Redmond, Mr Dillon, and Mr Devlin) would be a poor and mean Government, and instead of prosperity there would be poverty, a depleted Exchequer, heavy taxation, jobbery, bigotry. Above all, instead of order there would be disorder.'[18] Against such a fate there could be no safeguards and any that were incorporated in the Bill would prove worthless.

'Civil and religious liberty' would also be casualties. Roman Catholic states were still perceived to be authoritarian and hierarchical, happy to restrict individual liberty through censorship and sectarian legislation. Home Rule would mean Rome Rule and the recent *Ne Temere* Decree regarding mixed marriages, applied to Ireland in 1908 despite the anguished opposition of all the reformed churches (and notwithstanding the precepts of the existing constitution), boded ill for a future under Roman Catholic authority. The Decree caused exceptional public outcry not only because of its insistence that marriages between Catholics and Protestants could only be solemnised by a Catholic priest, with its implication that Protestant ministers were not Christian, but more especially because such a marriage could only be undertaken at all if both parties promised in advance that all children of their union would be brought up as Catholics. In a country where Protestants found themselves in a minority and where mixed marriages were not uncommon, this requirement could only weaken further their relative position. But it would upset also the existing convention whereby the sons of such unions followed the religion of their father and daughters that of their mother: a convention that preserved land and property within the same denomination from one generation to the next.

Ignoring the fact that it had been a Protestant government that had imposed penal legislation on Catholics in Ireland in the seventeenth and eighteenth centuries, Protestants looked to the traditional view of toleration and liberty of conscience associated with the Glorious Revolution and determined to uphold their existing rights, based on their citizenship of a United and Protestant Kingdom.

And there was no point referring to the terms of this bill that limited so heavily the responsibilities of the proposed Dublin parliament. William Pitt had concluded in 1800 that Union was the only alternative to a complete rupture. And Ulster's own leader, Sir Edward Carson, now put it in a nutshell once again: 'There can be no permanent resting place between complete Union and total separation'.[19] Whatever was said of this Bill, it breached the Union and would lead straight to an independent Ireland.

Here then is the source of the passion aroused by this modest measure. Redmond might argue with sincerity that he was satisfied with its mild devolutionary powers, but Unionists saw it only as the first step down a slippery slope which, once embarked upon, could brook no going back. Their struggle was a zero-sum encounter where no compromise was possible. Their winner-takes-all stance and the fact that the bitter hostility between Protestant and Catholic was of such long standing are the keys to attitudes struck then and maintained since. It is hard to effect reconciliation and compromise when one side feels that its entire case hangs or falls as a totality. To both sides, national allegiance was at stake and, to both sides, allegiance was possible only to one state.

To the devout man, guiding principles can be seen as a bundle of sticks tightly tied together. Let one go and the whole bundle is loosened and fatally weakened. This is the theology of beleaguered Protestantism. It begets the politics of 'Not an Inch'.

2

NO COMPROMISE: 1913–18

The Unionists of Ulster, led by Sir Edward Carson and his able local henchman James Craig, did not rest on their laurels. They formed their own defence organisation, the Ulster Volunteer Force; raised money and arms, planned a separate government should Home Rule be enacted; and renewed the passion and commitment of their allies in Britain, both political and military. At first determined to stop Home Rule of any sort, they watched their Conservative partners accept, by June 1912, that some such measure was unstoppable, and by late December 1912 had themselves recognised its inevitability. Thenceforward their aim was to exclude the maximum amount of territory in the north of Ireland commensurate with their own safety.

Would that area be nine-county Ulster or some lesser area? Carson's proposal of nine counties was rejected by Asquith in January 1913. His later suggestion of a six-county bloc, first mooted privately in the autumn of 1913, was turned by the government early in March 1914 into a proposal for a temporary measure, but this Carson himself rejected with contempt: 'We do not want sentence of death with a stay of execution for six years.'[1] Carson made this as a final offer, again, in July 1914 at the abortive Buckingham Palace Conference, to a frustrated and increasingly anxious Redmond, but by then too many reverses had been suffered by the government and their Home Rule allies for Redmond to compromise and no agreement was reached. A nine-county exclusion would be proposed again but from this point onwards the six-county suggestion was to find increasing favour.

Civil war in Ireland was looming when, on 4 August 1914, the greater catastrophe of war with Germany broke out. The Home Rule Act was made law on 18 September, despite Conservative anger, but it was postponed from coming into effect by a Suspensory Act 'for twelve months, or such later date (not being later than the end of the present war) as may be fixed by His Majesty by Order in Council'.[2] Asquith also promised that separate provision would be made for 'Ulster' (undefined) before Home Rule became operative.[3]

Internal conflict was averted. Armed Protestant Unionists and armed Catholic Nationalists moved to the Continent side by side, the one to preserve loyal Ulster for the Union, the other to secure the rights of small nations in general and in particular to ensure that the promise of Home Rule for Ireland would be honoured.

That this response occurred was to some extent a tribute to the respective leaders, Carson and Redmond. In a letter to *The Times*, on 1 August 1914, Carson urged the bulk of the Ulster Volunteer Force to make ready to guard Ireland, while others should prepare to fight abroad; Redmond, in an emotional speech in the Commons on 3 August, committed the Irish Volunteers to the defence of their country, thus allowing regular troops to leave for France. With Home Rule on the Statute Book on 18 September, he went further two days later, in a speech at Woodenbridge, in his home county of Wicklow, encouraging volunteers to account for themselves 'as men, not only in Ireland itself, but wherever the fighting line extends'.[4]

This policy was to cause an immediate split in the Irish Volunteers, the great majority of their 180,000 members backing Redmond, but a hard core of more extreme nationalists, around 12,000 strong, withdrawing to ensure that there remained in Ireland a dedicated body capable of guarding against future British perfidy. Redmond had taken a gamble but he had a vision by which to justify it. He sought to earn the gratitude of English public opinion, and to be prepared and trained should unforeseen hitches occur, but above all he hoped that his Irishmen might find themselves fighting alongside Carson's, already some way further down the road of acceptance into the British army, for, he argued, 'This is the way to end the unhappiness and discords and confusion of Ireland. Let Irish men come together in the trenches and spill their blood together and I say there is no power on earth when they come home can induce them to turn as enemies one upon the other.'[5]

Redmond and Carson alike had encountered the hostility of Lord Kitchener, made Minister of War on 5 August, when they went separately to see him on 7th. Kitchener was not impressed by 'irregular militias'[6] did not like politicians and was inclined to turn both offers away. The reduced state of his forces and the necessity of speedy recruitment induced him to alter his tune, however, and as the UVF, then about 85,000 strong, was already disciplined, trained and to a large extent equipped, steps were taken to bring in a solid mass of its members, with their own officers and insignia, and with privileged recruiting arrangements, to form the 36th (Ulster) Division.

Although matters were handled very differently in regard to Redmond's less trained and equipped followers, eventually the 16th (Irish) Division did in some measure realise his dream. For his volunteers, however, things from the beginning were less simple and in the eighteen months from August 1914 to February 1916 recruiting patterns reflected both the motivation of individuals and the methods of the recruiters. UVF members joined up more quickly and proportionately in greater numbers, but the greatest number of recruits from Ireland in this period, some 48,000 of the 95,000 involved, had no Volunteer affiliation, compared with 25,000 from the UVF and 22,000 from Redmond's National Volunteers. The split, the disruption of recruitment, and the widespread reluctance to be called to fight overseas, which further diminished the popularity of the National Volunteers, meant that their numbers fell away and their effectiveness disappeared. Sadly, it was observed, 'The review of 27,000 National Volunteers at Phoenix Park, Dublin, in Easter 1915, was their last national display of any numerical strength.'[7]

During these first years of the war, the leaders of Nationalist and of Unionist Ireland also responded differently to the opportunities of office. Redmond, by his honourable if over-rigid adherence to a policy of aloofness from government and position, and by the silence he loyally maintained despite rebuffs on every side from the War Office, cut himself off from the openings that the conflict presented. In May 1915, for example, when dissatisfaction with the way the war was being waged forced Asquith to broaden his government into a coalition with the Conservatives and even with a representative of Labour, the Liberal leader sought also to include both Irishmen. Redmond refused, but Carson, threatened only the year before with charges of treason, felt no such inhibition and accepted the post of Attorney General! Although he resigned in October 1915, in continuing dissatisfaction with Asquith's war management, he returned again in December as First Lord of the Admiralty in Lloyd George's successor Ministry, moving to the inner War Cabinet in July 1917, before his final resignation in January 1918. At each reshuffle, furthermore, Conservative and Unionist power grew, while Asquith and his followers, the majority of the old Liberal allies of the Irish, went into opposition. In the competition for public recognition in Britain, the Ulster Unionists were pulling ahead. Their favourable image had been enhanced by further events in 1916.

The explanation for these events must be sought in peripheral areas, away from the limelight, and amongst those who had never accepted Home Rule or who, even before the war broke out, had expressed themselves dissatisfied with the terms of the 1912 Bill as promulgated. A ballad of the time expressed the mood of disenchantment:

> Is it this you call Home Rule?.
> Do you take me for a fool?
> . . . .
> All your promises were vain
> So I'm turning to Sinn Fein[8]

Arthur Griffith's Sinn Fein was the logical movement to which to turn from Redmond's party, yet it was not Sinn Fein that was determined to use the war, England's present 'difficulty', as Ireland's latest 'opportunity'. The outbreak of

European hostilities was just what the more active members of the IRB had been waiting for. It was they who had taken a leading part in creating the Irish Volunteers in November 1913, inspired by the example of their Ulster opponents in the January of that year. The very success of their initiative had in turn alarmed the leaders of parliamentary nationalism into demanding a dominant role in the command structure of what might soon become the militia of Home Rule Ireland. Redmond's demand to place twenty-five nominees on the ruling committee of the Volunteers, in June 1914, came at an awkward time, for guns, purchased in Germany, were then on the high sea and rejection of this demand might have led to the disintegration and impotence of the force. Redmond had his way, therefore, but the original members of this ruling committee were those who organised the split in September 1914, after Redmond's call for overseas service. They met together, expelled Redmond's nominees, keeping the Irish Volunteer name for themselves, and expressing no regrets that the bulk of the movement followed Redmond, to be known thereafter as the Irish National or Redmond Volunteers.

The IRB, and those respectable non-IRB leaders, such as Eoin MacNeill, whose patriotism had first led them to oppose armed unionism with armed nationalism, were content to have the disciplined and dedicated core of the movement, however small. They would remain in readiness in Ireland to uphold Home Rule after the war, or resist any effort to conscript Irishmen during it. Irish Volunteers owed allegiance only to Ireland, they argued, and could wage war at the behest only of an Irish National Government. The IRB, however, was quick to add in secret to this agenda: to plan, in consultation with their American contacts, an armed insurrection during the war, with a view to winning an Irish Republic, if not immediately, then through such action being recognised at the post-war peace negotiations.

IRB numbers were still small at the outbreak of war – perhaps no more than 1600–1700 in the whole country – but they were well placed, as the creation and control of the Irish Volunteers indicated. Their infiltration of the Gaelic League was to lead to a take-over of its executive in 1915, to provide further evidence of their manipulative success. The war also enabled the younger activists to push aside the IRB constitution's commitment to revolution only when the country demanded it, and to organise an uprising without the knowledge of the official leadership of the Volunteers.

Tom Clarke and Sean MacDermott found themselves masters of the IRB between meetings of the Supreme Council and it was on their initiative that a secret meeting was held with other activists in September 1914: with Labour, represented by James Connolly and the Trade Unionist William O'Brien; with Arthur Griffith of Sinn Fein; and with other influential IRB men such as John MacBride, Sean T. O'Kelly and Sean McGarry, and younger enthusiasts such as Patrick Pearse, Thomas MacDonagh, Joseph Plunkett and Eamon Ceannt. From this meeting, which resolved to reconvene but never did, a strategy emerged that the IRB alone continued to develop: to give assistance to German forces landing in Ireland (providing guarantees were given to help win Irish independence); to oppose with force any attempt by the government to impose conscription or to disarm the volunteers; to stage a rising before the war ended to proclaim the freedom of Ireland, and thus to establish Ireland's right to advance its national cause after the war. At the same time they would build up the Volunteers, the Fianna youth movement and the separate women's organisation, Cumann na mBan, in preparation for action.

In May 1915 the IRB established a military council, consisting of Pearse, Plunkett and Ceannt, none as yet on the Supreme Council, though Pearse was to be co-opted onto it in August. In September MacDermott and Clarke were added, and in January and April 1916, James Connolly (the outstanding labour figure who was at that moment threatening to make his own gesture with the small Citizen Army that he controlled) and Thomas MacDonagh, respectively. It was these seven men, forming what had become known as the Military Council of the IRB, who planned the rising. No date was as yet fixed and the non-IRB leaders of the Volunteers, such as Eoin MacNeill and The O'Rahilly, were kept in the dark, and even Bulmer Hobson, for these men were known to favour military action only when a fair chance of success might be expected; otherwise keeping the Volunteers intact was their priority.

Attempts were made to obtain supplies from Germany, and the agreement of the German authorities to send a shipload of arms, combined with their own fear of a peace deal being struck between the belligerents before they could act, were probably crucial to the decision to stage their rising at Easter 1916. But the fact of that event, from Monday 24 April 1916 to Sunday 30th, was to have great repercussion upon Ireland's development, not least upon its divided peoples. Confused and acrimonious though its calling may have been, and almost wholly confined to Dublin though it was, the Easter Rising proclaimed the Irish Republic and defended it in arms, to the death for many. Its aftermath of execution, imprisonment and martial law, the continuation of the war and the renewed horrors, the political changes and the resentments and threats that it brought in its train contributed to a hardening of attitudes throughout Ireland. By its end the stakes had been raised; and the divisions made deeper.

Patrick Pearse had emerged as the Commander in Chief of the rebel force (numbering no more than 1,600, including the 219 Citizen Army contingent) as well as Chairman of the Provisional Government, whose Proclamation of the Irish Republic he read out that Easter Monday morning. The Republic thus proclaimed looked to history for its justification, and, despite some reservations later revealed, put its faith in the republican ideal. It claimed 'the allegiance of every Irishman and Irishwoman' and its short statement included a description of its aims and scope.[9]

But, as Roy Foster has observed, there was another characteristic of the young men who carried through their fateful dream that Easter, and this was their poetic identification of 'the Irish soul as Catholic and Gaelic'.[10] And for all the declared commitment to the good of all, this characteristic had been expressed frequently in prose and

POBLACHT NA H EIREANN.

THE PROVISIONAL GOVERNMENT

OF THE

IRISH REPUBLIC

TO THE PEOPLE OF IRELAND.

IRISHMEN AND IRISHWOMEN : In the name of God and of the dead generations from which she receives her old tradition of nationhood, Ireland, through us, summons her children to her flag and strikes for her freedom.

Having organised and trained her manhood through her secret revolutionary organisation, the Irish Republican Brotherhood, and through her open military organisations, the Irish Volunteers and the Irish Citizen Army, having patiently perfected her discipline, having resolutely waited for the right moment to reveal itself, she now seizes that moment, and, supported by her exiled children in America and by gallant allies in Europe, but relying in the first on her own strength, she strikes in full confidence of victory.

We declare the right of the people of Ireland to the ownership of Ireland, and to the unfettered control of Irish destinies, to be sovereign and indefeasible. The long usurpation of that right by a foreign people and government has not extinguished the right, nor can it ever be extinguished except by the destruction of the Irish people. In every generation the Irish people have asserted their right to national freedom and sovereignty : six times during the past three hundred years they have asserted it in arms. Standing on that fundamental right and again asserting it in arms in the face of the world, we hereby proclaim the Irish Republic as a Sovereign Independent State, and we pledge our lives and the lives of our comrades-in-arms to the cause of its freedom, of its welfare; and of its exaltation among the nations.

The Irish Republic is entitled to, and hereby claims, the allegiance of every Irishman and Irishwoman. The Republic guarantees religious and civil liberty, equal rights and equal opportunities to all its citizens, and declares its resolve to pursue the happiness and prosperity of the whole nation and of all its parts, cherishing all the children of the nation equally, and oblivious of the differences carefully fostered by an alien government, which have divided a minority from the majority in the past.

Until our arms have brought the opportune moment for the establishment of a permanent National Government, representative of the whole people of Ireland and elected by the suffrages of all her men and women, the Provisional Government, hereby constituted, will administer the civil and military affairs of the Republic in trust for the people.

We place the cause of the Irish Republic under the protection of the Most High God, Whose blessing we invoke upon our arms, and we pray that no one who serves that cause will dishonour it by cowardice, inhumanity, or rapine. In this supreme hour the Irish nation must, by its valour and discipline and by the readiness of its children to sacrifice themselves for the common good, prove itself worthy of the august destiny to which it is called.

Signed on Behalf of the Provisional Government,

THOMAS J. CLARKE.

SEAN Mac DIARMADA. THOMAS MacDONAGH.
P. H. PEARSE. EAMONN CEANNT,
JAMES CONNOLLY. JOSEPH PLUNKETT

A facsimile reproduction of the Republican Proclamation issued on Easter Monday, 1916

poetry, in Irish and in English, in the preceding months. The very fact and the timing of the Rising were also utterly careless of the susceptibilities of those fighting a war to preserve the United Kingdom, and their British heritage within both Union and Empire.

Reactions to this armed uprising were swift, various and volatile. In Ireland the military authorities, under Major-General Sir John Maxwell, who arrived to take command only on 28 April, subdued the rebels by superior numbers and fire-power and rounded up as many of their suspected supporters as could be located. Martial law was proclaimed and the principal rebels were quickly tried by courts martial, ninety being condemned to death. Between 3 and 12 May fifteen of these sentences were carried out by shooting, before a halt was called, a sixteenth being added on 3 August when Roger Casement, a distinguished former diplomat, was hanged at Pentonville prison for his efforts to raise recruits for the cause amongst captured Irish troops in Germany. In time revulsion at these executions and admiration for the bravery and sincerity of the insurgents, as more information became available, made their own contribution to a swing of public opinion, but the most obvious local Irish reactions at the time were the horror of the Dublin middle classes at this stab in Redmond's back, and the glee of Dublin's poor, who indulged in joyous looting on a considerable scale.

Redmond, in London during these events, expressed his and the Party's outrage and regret, but his deputy, John Dillon, confined to his house in North Great George's Street near the Dublin city centre, was more closely attuned to the public mood and quickly warned against both hasty political condemnation and harsh military retribution.

In Unionist circles in Ulster, reactions were mixed. There was no division on the matter of outraged condemnation: the *Belfast Telegraph*'s dismissal of the 'parcel of frothy ranters' who had dared to challenge the British Empire was echoed by the *Fermanagh Times*, which had 'not language sufficiently powerful to denounce adequately this Sinn Fein betrayal of every reputable element of citizenship'.[11] Initially, in contrast, some

Unionists were inclined to welcome the fact that the dastardly nationalists had at last revealed themselves for what they were. Belfast businessman Adam Duffin, for example, writing to his daughter on Tuesday 25 April, felt it was 'good business its having come to a head'.[12] But the certainty that the government could no longer have any truck with such traitors soon gave way to a horrified realisation that, on the contrary, the events of Easter Week had convinced the government that concessions must be made. Ulster loyalists soon absorbed the message that Irish nationalism, derided as a figment before, had an essential reality, and when John Dillon rose in the Commons on 11 May to defend the insurgents he confirmed their worst suspicions. The entire nationalist movement stood condemned, justifying, in the words of Ronald McNeill, MP, 'the whole basis of Ulster's unchanging attitude towards Nationalism'.[13] Less than two months after the true face of this phenomenon had revealed itself, Sir Edward Carson was persuading a stunned Ulster Unionist Council to agree to the immediate implementation of Home Rule for Ireland, save for the six north-eastern counties of Ulster, the maximum area that could permanently be excluded.

The government, bogged down in the war and anxious to bring in as an ally an America notoriously interested in Irish affairs, responded promptly to the Easter Rising. Asquith visited Ireland from 12 to 17 May and on return to London gave to Lloyd George the responsibility of bringing in a settlement. Lloyd George negotiated separately with Redmond and Carson, promising the former verbally that his proposal to exclude six northern counties would be but temporary. To Carson, however, he was forced to commit to paper a promise that they 'would not be included unless at some future time the Imperial Parliament passes an Act for that purpose'.[14] And it was this reassurance that enabled the Ulster leader to recommend acceptance of the scheme, in the interests of an Empire at war and in the firm conviction that if the Home Rule Act was to be implemented at the end of hostilities it was unlikely that a better deal could be struck, and then perhaps only after considerable effort. A reluctant Council, while reiterating its 'unabated abhorrence of the policy of Home Rule', and reserving to itself 'complete freedom of action in the future'[15] should the present negotiations prove abortive, gave Sir Edward a free hand to conclude an agreement with the Cabinet. The eventual agreement foundered in the Lords in July, when the 'permanent and enduring'[16] nature of the exclusion was calmly asserted by Lord Lansdowne, who also poured scorn on Redmond's pretensions in regard to matters of defence. Redmond, humiliated and discredited, quickly washed his hands of the affair. Home Rule remained suspended, with its adherents diminished in Nationalist eyes.

Other factors contributed to the rise of alternative, more extreme nationalism, and in opposition more determined Unionism, during the remainder of the war. Not least of these in regard to the latter was the heroic sacrifice demanded of British troops at the Somme in that summer of 1916. There were Irishmen amongst those troops, Irishmen from many quarters and all religious persuasions, but the most visible and cohesive group of those called to lay down their lives was the 36th (Ulster) Division, and the nobility and the enormity of their commitment entered deeply into the Ulster Unionist memory. Here was a blood sacrifice far greater and in a mightier cause than that offered up in Dublin. And in the years to come, the anniversaries and jubilees of the one would be paralleled by those of the other in sharp and perpetual contrast.

The government could not let Ireland drift for long. Again responding to American pressure, this time from the London ambassador of an ally that had entered the war in April 1917, Lloyd George, who had replaced Asquith as Prime Minister early the previous December, agreed to establish a Convention of leading Irishmen to seek a way forward. Southern Unionists, only too aware now just where their northern brethren stood, sought terms with the Home Rule Party in an effort to keep Ireland united and within the Union. Ulster Unionists, at the Convention largely in a watching capacity, made no constructive contribution and were unmoved by its eventual failure, in April 1918. By then Redmond had died, on 6 March 1918, to be replaced as leader by Dillon; and the inheritors of the Rising, who had boycotted the Convention with disdain, had consolidated their position.

Strangely, for Arthur Griffith's Sinn Fein Party had not participated in the events of Easter Week, the Rising had been widely attributed to it. Sinn Fein was the handiest portmanteau description for extreme nationalism and was accepted by press, people and government without question. In October 1917 the reorganising remnants of the IRB, the Volunteers, and Sinn Fein itself met, in their own Convention, to put matters right and to unite under one banner. Already the backlash of sympathy for the insurgents had combined with repudiation of the humiliated Party to bring four by-election victories that year to Sinn Fein. Now, a thousand delegates representing republican and non-republican separatists, physical-force men and the non-physical-force tradition, placed themselves under the leadership of Eamon de Valera, the senior survivor of the Rising, and committed themselves to securing 'international recognition of Ireland as an independent Irish Republic'. Arthur Griffith was content to take second place, especially as it had been agreed in advance that, having achieved republican status: 'The Irish people may by referendum freely choose their own form of government.'[17]

In November, de Valera was elected President of the Irish Volunteers, uniting the civil and military leadership, though there was still much IRB manipulation behind the scenes, new activists, such as Michael Collins and Diarmuid Lynch, joining older hands such as Sean McGarry in senior posts. The baton of dynamic nationalism had been passed on, as would soon be apparent as the European war entered its final phase.

Conscription had been an issue with regard to Ireland ever since it had been first introduced in Britain in 1916, when Carson had been amongst its most ardent devotees. The great German offensive of March 1918 faced the government once more with an urgent manpower need, and, willing to extend the conscription age span in Britain, it decided at last to take power to apply the measure to Ireland, by Order in Council, when the moment seemed right. The Bill to grant such power was introduced to parliament on 10 April and, in the teeth of unanimous Irish Party opposition, was made law on 16 April. Chief Secretary Greenwood had opined to Lloyd George that he 'might almost as well recruit Germans'[18] as apply conscription to Ireland, and even Carson, again out of the Cabinet and at the head of the Ulster Unionists, had warned that the disturbances that would arise meant the measure was not worth contemplating, but in the event the impact on Nationalist Ireland was to prove crucial.

In despair of ever influencing policy, Dillon and his followers withdrew from Westminster and returned to Dublin to join with the rest of the country's Nationalist representatives to oppose the application of this new power to conscript Irishmen. Dillon and his lieutenants were to share platforms with leading Churchmen and Sinn Feiners in apparent equality, but the very stratagem of withdrawal from Westminster was a Sinn Fein policy, and the Party's record of support of recruiting in the past had not been forgotten. From this point onwards Sinn Fein, proscribed by the new military Viceroy, Lord French, on 18 May 1918, but despite or perhaps because of this, winning the East Cavan by-election on 21 June, made the political running. The fact that all nationalists, the Catholic Church prominent amongst them, stood together in common 'disloyalty' simply confirmed the disgust in which Northern Unionists had come to view them. The fact that conscription, though never in fact applied, remained a threat up to the end of the war, does much to explain the success of Sinn Fein in the General Election that was held just a month after its end.

The general election of December 1918, the last held on an all-Ireland basis, revealed the extent to which Irishmen had moved away from a devolved Home Rule solution within the jurisdiction of the Imperial parliament. Its voting statistics have been analysed to support very different positions, the more possible because of the many uncontested constituencies and because the extended franchise and the length of time that had elapsed since the previous election at the end of 1910 permitted much theorising about first-time voters. But one incontrovertible fact to set beside Sinn Fein's remarkable victory was the solidity of Unionist opposition to it in the north-east of the country. Sweeping the Parliamentary Party aside by 73 seats to 6 (4 of which were by agreement with Sinn Fein in Ulster to avoid splitting the non-Unionist vote), Sinn Fein were opposed by 26 Unionists, of whom all but 3 (including 2 for Dublin University) were in Ulster: a solid phalanx of determined opponents denying Sinn Fein's right to speak for Ireland. The age-old division within Ireland, now more sharply than ever posited in religious and cultural terms, had become more clearly defined also in geographical location.

3

DIVISION AND RETRENCHMENT:
1919–25

The general election in 1918, which in Ireland resulted in a triumph for Sinn Fein, in the United Kingdom as a whole saw renewed confidence placed in Lloyd George's wartime coalition. Indeed the government was returned with an overwhelming majority and with a huge preponderance of Conservative members. The Commons was to be left even more unbalanced when the Sinn Fein MPs adhered to their electoral promise and, disdaining to appear at Westminster, created their own assembly, Dail Eireann, in Dublin, and set about building an alternative administration for Ireland.

Lloyd George had sought the support of the electorate to enable him to win the peace, as he had won the war, and he thus gave priority to this complex task, the international negotiations preoccupying him and his leading Ministers throughout much of 1919. As the series of Peace Treaties neared completion, however, so time began to run out in which to implement the Home Rule Act of 1914. Something would have to be done to resolve the Irish 'quarrel' which had so steadfastly outlasted the 'cataclysm' of the Great War.[1]

To this end a Cabinet Committee was established in October 1919, under the chairmanship of Walter Long, former leader of the Ulster Unionists and a stalwart champion still of their cause. Towards the end of December a plan had been formulated. It was to emerge as the Government of Ireland Act, 1920. It was, in effect, a fourth Home Rule Bill, and it reflected the tense debate over exclusion that had characterised the Home Rule issue since the Committee stage of the third bill, in June 1912. It also reflected the Conservative domination of the Coalition Government and the fact that the Ulster Unionists, thanks to the withdrawal of Sinn Fein and the annihilation of the Irish Parliamentary Party, were the dominant representatives of Ireland in the Commons.

The Long Committees response to the need to make special provision for Ulster was to recommend not one but two Home Rule parliaments for Ireland. It was already clear that Nationalist Ireland now sought something far beyond Home Rule: even the Home Rulers had pitched their claim well beyond the 1914 Act in their attempt to win the election in 1918 and Ulster Unionists wished only to remain a part of the United Kingdom on the same basis as the rest of their fellow citizens. But the Committee felt that it would be best to withdraw direct British rule from all of Ireland, thus minimising the gravity of its partition into two jurisdictions. And to emphasise a long-term commitment to Irish unity, it recommended the establishment of a Council of Ireland to which each devolved government could transfer powers, as relationships improved, so that a single, devolved Irish parliament might eventually be formed.

But for what area would the second Home Rule parliament be responsible? Walter Long favoured the nine counties of Ulster: a recognised unit, with a strong Nationalist minority that would not easily be ignored. It became clear after consultation with the Unionist leaders, however, that if they were to have a local parliament thrust upon them then they preferred to administer the six north-eastern counties, with the very safe majority that would entail. (Four counties would have been safer still but Ulster and English Unionists alike thought this too small to justify parliamentary institutions and the former were unwilling to abandon substantial Unionist communities in Fermanagh and Tyrone.) The government decided, accordingly, that it was better to have at least some Irishmen willing to work its scheme, and in the adjournment debate before Christmas, on 22 December, 1919, Lloyd George outlined his proposals. The six-county area was indicated but it was emphasised that no final decision had yet been taken.

The Cabinet did not commit itself to such a decision, so crucial to the future of Ireland, until 24 February 1920, the day before the bill was introduced to parliament. The 'Partition Bill' (see Appendix A) was a long and complex one, stressing that Westminster's supremacy was to continue 'unaffected and undiminished over all persons and things in Ireland and every part thereof', and dividing Ireland into two unequal parts: 'Northern Ireland', defined as 'the six parliamentary counties of Antrim, Armagh, Down, Fermanagh, Londonderry and Tyrone, and the parliamentary boroughs of Belfast and Londonderry'; and 'Southern Ireland', defined as the rest of the island.[2] Ironically, given that in the end it was to be implemented only by the loyalists of the North, it was filled with restrictions and reservations, reflecting the prevalent distrust of nationalist Ireland. It was to occasion powerful debate outside parliament as well as within, and not the least of these debates occurred in Belfast where the Ulster Unionist Council, finally consulted in March, witnessed a spirited attempt by nine-county exclusionists to reverse the area agreement.

The decision of this Council Meeting, reached on 10 March, was to confirm the six counties: the old Covenant of 1912 was brushed aside and, by a mere show of hands, the three rejected counties were 'thrown to the wolves'.[3] In a last-ditch effort to overturn this decision, on 27 May, nine-county supporters mustered only 80 out of a gathering of 390. These were fateful decisions, turning on passionate arguments. It was one thing, it was protested, to sacrifice three counties during the war in the interests of allied victory, but now, in peacetime, the old Unionist solidarity should be honoured. Eloquent statements,[4] about the established entity that was Ulster, its natural boundary, its trading links and communications networks, and above all its healthier balance of communities, which would still leave a viable Unionist majority in terms of seats and population, were ignored in favour of the maximum area deemed sufficient and safe.

That area did include Nationalist majorities in Fermanagh and Tyrone, and in the border towns of Londonderry and

Newry. Nationalists everywhere, but particularly in these areas, were dismayed by the terms of the Bill. Nationalists in the north, long under the shadow of 'separate provision for Ulster,' had been divided on whether they preferred, in the face of the inevitable, the exclusion of a large area with accompanying safety of numbers, or the smallest area that a Unionist majority would justify. Nationalists cut off in the east, in Belfast and in North Antrim, tended to favour the former; those in the majority nationalist counties the latter. All assumed a limited time period; all would have preferred continued direct rule from Westminster; none favoured a local parliament dominated by their traditional enemies.

The solution agreed between Unionists at Westminster, therefore, represented the worst of all worlds. It was one, furthermore, ill-designed to separate two peoples so that they could enjoy their different allegiances in peace. As J. J. Lee has observed, 'Partition had long existed in the mind. Now it existed on the map. But what a map!' Trenchantly he has listed the anomalies, pointing out that there were some areas of greater Unionist strength outside Belfast's jurisdiction than within, for example in North Monaghan compared with South Armagh, while 'the Catholic majorities in Fermanagh and Tyrone were bigger than the Protestant majorities in Londonderry and Armagh'.[5]

All over Europe, in these years, boundary commissions were endeavouring to sort out untidy peoples into new states. The decision to go for a clean-cut, six-county exclusion may have seemed to the government at that time to be the simplest, the least troublesome. It did not bode well for the future, however, and even at the hour of its implementation it was to be circumscribed by violent events.

Sinn Fein, having embarked on its own attempt to establish control of Ireland, dismissed this British legislation with contempt. Unionists, now led by Sir James Craig, might complain that they had not asked for a Home Rule parliament, might refuse to vote for it, and might accept it only as 'a supreme sacrifice'[6] in the interests of peace, but they soon realised its advantages and they were quick to implement its terms and seek security in its institutions. Given the royal assent in December 1920, the Act decreed an election timetable for the spring of 1921. But while Unionists prepared for this innovation, Nationalists pressed on towards a different goal. They had already established Dail Eireann in Dublin on 21 January 1919. By coincidence, guerrilla warfare commenced in Tipperary on the very same day. It began modestly but soon escalated into a series of bloodthirsty exchanges with Crown forces, and further reinforced Ulster Unionists in their determination to have nothing to do with the rest of Ireland. They were to find much trouble on their own doorstep, however, before the security they sought could be achieved.

By legislation, then, Ireland was partitioned in 1920. Redmond had resisted this move and had striven to reduce Unionist pretensions. The Sinn Fein leaders rejected Westminster and pursued complete, all-Ireland independence in defiance of it. They dismissed the 1920 Act but took advantage of its electoral machinery, North and South, to renew their mandate, the Second Dail Eireann convening on 16 August 1921. By then the Northern Ireland parliament had been opened by King George V, Northern Unionists had been catered for, and the government had inclined towards cutting its losses in the rest of Ireland. Britain's reputation had, it felt, become tarnished by the brutalities of the Anglo-Irish struggle; American and Dominion opinion had grown restive; costs in men and money had mounted; Labour, Liberal, religious and trade union opinion at home had increasingly demanded a negotiated settlement. So Eamon de Valera, at last identified by Lloyd George as a credible leader with whom to do business, had been summoned to London, after a truce had been agreed from 11 July. De Valera had proceeded to reject the British offer of dominion status, qualified as it was in significant ways and with the requirement that Northern Ireland's powers should remain for as long as its people wished, and this rejection had been confirmed, as a final act of defiance, by the First Dail Cabinet.

Now, and especially after the Second Dail had unanimously confirmed rejection of Lloyd George's latest communication, reported to its members by de Valera on 17 August, it looked as if no radical settlement could be reached. In Belfast there was relief. On 20 September, Craig was able to express his determination 'to work in friendly rivalry' with his 'fellow countrymen in the South and West' (presumably in the hoped-for government of Southern Ireland) and 'to vie with them in the government of the people, to vie with them in the markets of the world'.[7] But it was not to be. Somehow Lloyd George and de Valera kept up a correspondence into the autumn until it was agreed that negotiations could begin to 'ascertain how the association of Ireland with the community of nations known as the British Empire might best be reconciled with Irish national aspirations'.[8] These negotiations threatened to jeopardise what had so recently been enacted at Westminster. There were to be anxious moments yet awhile for Ulster Unionists.

From 11 October to 6 December two teams of plenipotentiaries strove to reconcile the irreconcilable: to square an independent all-Ireland Republic with the allegiance of Ireland to the Crown, non-coercion of Northern Ireland, and the defence provisions needed for the security of the United Kingdom. The Irish, led by Arthur Griffith, strongly backed by Michael Collins, sought both in-dependence and unity, and they were determined, should a breakdown occur, that it would be on the latter, and not on an issue of status that world opinion might have difficulty in grasping. Lloyd George, experienced negotiator that he was, realised the Irish priorities and worked skilfully to counter them. In his turn, though he was not averse to putting pressure on the Unionists along the way, he strove to maintain Ireland within the King's dominions and, for at the last resort he was dependent on Conservative support, to ensure Northern Ireland's survival.

James Craig, now Prime Minister of Northern Ireland, though not yet in receipt from Westminster of all the powers necessary for his government to function, refused to be a party to the negotiations. He had courageously travelled to a secret meeting with de Valera in May 1921 to try to gain recognition from Sinn Fein of Northern Ireland's rights, but there had been no meeting of minds. Now he denied the Irish leader's claim, and that of his plenipotentiaries, to speak for Ireland as a whole. Technically, Northern Ireland was represented by Lloyd George and his colleagues, but the pressure put on Craig to accept Irish unity, with devolved powers from Dublin rather than London, greatly antagonised the Ulster leader and his Cabinet, and did much to reinforce their determination to get their administration up and running, as a defence against possible future London perfidy as much as against that which they feared from Dublin. Later on, they were to claim more than once that as they 'were not a party to the agreement' they 'would refuse to be bound by any decision that might be arrived at'.[9]

In the event, through a mixture of concessions, threats and ambiguities, agreement was reached on 6 December (see Appendix B), though the resulting 'Treaty' was to lead to civil war in the Irish Free State, the almost independent Dominion successor to 'Southern Ireland' that emerged from the process. The Irish Free State, given the same constitutional status as Canada (a device that avoided definition of 'dominion status' at a time when it was evolving towards complete sovereignty) was retained within the Empire/Commonwealth, Britain's defence needs were met, and Northern Ireland was permitted to emerge unscathed.

Or so, at least, it was argued. But here the greatest and most crucial ambiguity in the Treaty came into play. The Treaty, or 'Articles of Agreement for a Treaty', to be precise, was concluded between 'Great Britain and Ireland', recognition, of a kind, of Sinn Fein's claim to unity. Northern Ireland's position was acknowledged, however, and its government was given the opportunity to opt out from the provisions of the Treaty and so to retain its relationship with London. But if it did so, and this was the ambiguous rub, it would have to submit itself to a Boundary Commission, which would redraw its frontiers 'in accordance with the wishes of the inhabitants, so far as may be compatible with economic and geographic conditions'.[10] Did this mean a mere frontier-tidying exercise or could such dramatic changes be wrought that Northern Ireland would cease to exist as a viable entity and be forced to throw in its lot with the Free State?

Craig and his Cabinet were not pleased that the previous year's 'final settlement'[11] should be so cavalierly thrown open once more. Reassuring, minimalist interpretations might be offered by leading Conservatives in the subsequent parliamentary debate, but the Irish delegates preferred to hope that, having reduced Northern Ireland to 'Belfast and its back yard', the Boundary Commission would effectively restore Ireland's unity. The scene was set for a period of uncertainty.

The search for an alternative to the Boundary Commission, followed by civil war, and finally squabbles over constitutional niceties, combined to prolong this uncertainty until December 1925. In the intervening period further complications were introduced which in turn were to exacerbate division and render its reconciliation more difficult.

Once the Treaty had been accepted on 14 January 1922, by the narrow margin of seven votes, it was Griffith and Collins who took control of affairs in Dublin. Collins, as Head of the Provisional Government charged with the Treaty's implementation, soon set about reaching an accommodation over the frontier with Craig: better, they both felt, that two Irishmen reach an agreement than that a Commission, chaired by a foreigner, be called to do so. Craig, who had actually raised the possibility of a border rectification commission in December 1919, during the Cabinet preparation of the 1920 Act, was hopeful that Collins would agree to the sort of limited exercise he had in mind. His government was beset by sectarian violence, with deaths, woundings, and damage to property on a large scale, and with many citizens, mainly Catholic, being driven from their homes and their jobs. An agreement that would help stabilise things politically would be particularly welcome. Collins had his own problems in Dublin, was acutely aware of the need to protect Catholic interests in the North, and was in a hurry to show that his vision of the Treaty's potential for unity was correct.

A preliminary meeting in London on 21 January 1922 agreed procedures for decision-making and both men made conciliatory promises. When detailed arguments were advanced on 2 February in Dublin, however, the extent of their contrary assumptions became clear and the prospect of an agreement disappeared. As neither man had been able to deliver on his earlier promises, prospects look bleak, and a letter by Collins to *The Times* on 4 February, expressing bitter disappointment and withdrawing co-operation across a range of mutual concerns, boded ill for the future.

Surprisingly, with British prompting, the two men did manage to conclude a pact in London, on 30 March, both being still under enormous domestic pressure. They declared peace, promised intergovernmental co-operation and reiterated their willingness to find a solution to the frontier problem without recourse to the Boundary Commission. But this agreement, too, collapsed without producing results, the civil war in the Free State and the death of Collins putting paid to its hopes.

So the Boundary Commission clause in the Treaty lived on. It envisaged three Commissioners, one appointed by each Irish Government, and a neutral Chairman, to be appointed by the British Government. At first the Belfast authorities were inclined to take up their place, to nominate a willing Lord Carson, and to try to get 'such terms of reference as were possible to act as safeguards'.[12] But as the slide to civil war gathered pace in the Free State and as Collins and de Valera entered into an electoral pact on 20 May 1922, so Craig altered course to condemn the Commission and to refuse to have anything to do with it. As he explained his public outburst to that effect to an affronted Churchill:

> The Boundary Commission has been at the root of all evil. If you can picture loyalists on the Borderland being asked by us to hang on with their teeth for the safety of the Province, you can also picture their unspoken cry to us if we sacrifice our lives and our property for the sake of the Province are you going to assent to a Commission which may subsequently by a stroke of the pen take away the very area you now ask us to defend? You can also visualise

that this recent pact between Collins and de Valera alters the whole circumstances. Hitherto, you and I have been anticipating the Free Staters holding out against de Valera, sweeping the country at the forthcoming election and placing themselves in a strong position to maintain law and order, in a Free State within the ambit of the British Empire. Now we are confronted with a combination, as 4 is to 5, of out and out Republicans and Free Staters who, through Collins, reiterate that the Treaty is merely a stepping stone to a republic.[13]

So far as Ulster Unionists were concerned, there was little to choose between the 'Here-and-now republicans of Mr de Valera' and the 'By-and-by republicans of Griffith and Collins'. They wanted nothing to do with either of them.

But Craig could not kill the Commission by unilateral action, even though, as it turned out, he could delay it by his non-co-operation. The outbreak of open warfare in June 1922, the death of Griffith and the killing of Collins in August, and the assumption of responsibility for the successful prosecution of hostilities by W. T. Cosgrave, not to mention the fall of Lloyd George's Coalition in October 1922, combined to prevent further intergovernmental action during that year, though the formal ratification of the Treaty on 6 December did provide the occasion for the government of Northern Ireland to opt out from its terms. This it duly did on 7 December. The Boundary Commission was now ready to be invoked.

With the civil war ended, on 24 May 1923, Cosgrave was at last able to consider invoking it. On 20 July, therefore, he appointed his Cabinet colleague, Eoin MacNeill, as Free State Commissioner and asked Baldwin's Conservative government to initiate procedures at its end. It was at this point that Craig's lack of co-operation became effective, and his prevarication was to receive added strength from Britain's political instability over the next fifteen months. Correspondence was still being exchanged between Belfast and London when Baldwin lost the 6 December 1923 election. It continued under the first Labour Premier, Ramsay MacDonald, who entered office on 24 January, and meetings involving both Craig and Cosgrave were held in April and

May 1924, before, on 10 May, Craig finally gave formal notification to MacDonald of his refusal to appoint a Commissioner.

The British Government had already secured the agreement of the former Canadian Premier, Sir Robert Borden, to act as Chairman, but only if both parties were willing to co-operate. Now someone else had to be found and to this end Mr Justice Feetham of the South African Supreme Court was nominated on 5 June. But could London appoint also for Northern Ireland? When asked, the Judicial Committee of the Privy Council said no, in July. Thus, to enable it to make such an appointment, legislation was needed, and legislation, furthermore, incorporating a supplement to the Treaty, to be agreed by both the Dublin and London governments. Both were highly nervous of falling on this issue, but, on 30 September in Dublin, and 9 October in London, Acts were successfully passed. On 24 October, J. R. Fisher, a former editor of the *Northern Whig*, was appointed (it seems after consultation with Craig) to represent Northern Ireland. In the general election six days later the Conservatives were returned to power. The Boundary Commission convened for its first meeting on 6 November 1924.

The work of the Boundary Commission represents another saga in modern Irish history and its full story has no place here. The interpretation of the Treaty's Article 12 – 'full of ambiguity, full of grave and dangerous ambiguity',[14] as Lord Buckmaster had described it in the House of Lords in March 1922 – was to prove crucial, and in this regard Chairman Feetham was in no doubt. As the *Report*, suppressed at the time but introduced and published by Geoffrey Hand in 1969, makes clear, Feetham held that:

> no wholesale reconstruction of the map was contemplated by the proviso – the Commission is not to reconstitute the two territories but to settle the boundaries between them. Northern Ireland must, when the boundaries have been determined, still be recognisable as the same provincial entity; the changes made must not be so drastic as to destroy its identity or make it impossible for it to continue as a separate province of the United Kingdom, with

its own parliament and Government for provincial affairs under the Government of Ireland Act.[15]

And so it was to turn out. In the autumn of 1925, when the Commissioners had just completed the first draft of their work, a leak in a leading Conservative newspaper disclosed that its proposals were merely of the frontier-rectification variety. On 7 November the *Morning Post* reproduced an amended map (see Appendix C1), accurately 'guessing' that the tortuous six-county border would be straightened, and making the startling revelation that not only would small parcels of territory be transferred from North to South, but that there would be, also, some lesser transfers in the opposite direction. Could this be true? If so, then Dublin's hopes would be dashed and there would be a quite unacceptable loss of Free State citizens to Northern Ireland. Cosgrave acted quickly, MacNeill resigned from both Commission and Cabinet, and a flurry of meetings took place between government representatives from Dublin and London and finally Belfast.

The result was an Agreement (amending and supplementing the Articles of Agreement for a Treaty between Great Britain and Ireland) signed in London, on 3 December 1925 (see Appendix C2). Under the first of its terms, the boundary between Northern Ireland and the rest of Ireland was left as it was. Other clauses in the agreement offered a measure of compensation to the Free State, on the one hand, releasing it from any liability under Article 5 of the Treaty for its share of the public debt of the United Kingdom and for the payment of war pensions, and on the other hand placing upon it the liability for malicious damage done to property within its territory from the start of hostilities in January 1919. Finally, the powers of the Council of Ireland relating to Northern Ireland were transferred to the government of Northern Ireland and the two Irish governments agreed to meet together in the future to consider matters of common interest. In this regard, the Preamble to the Agreement also expressed the desire of the three governments 'to avoid any causes of friction which might mar or retard the further growth of friendly relations', and stressed their present 'spirit of friendly comradeship'.[16]

It was a most significant agreement. For Northern Ireland, a tripartite negotiation, this time including its own representatives, had reached a satisfactory conclusion and the Damoclean sword of territorial uncertainty had at last been removed. For the Irish Free State the same negotiation had produced bitter disappointment, to be followed by a period of anxiety as a storm of popular anger was weathered, though here too there was some relief from uncertainty, for the unquantified financial obligation of Article 5 had already caused difficulties in the pursuit of international loans. For both governments, in the event, the agreement forced a not unwelcome facing up to reality: division did exist in Ireland and if it was ever to be removed it would have to be by a process of co-operation and understanding. The Craig and Cosgrave administrations could bear this in mind as they turned to the pressing internal problems that faced them, the one struggling to rebuild a state ravaged by civil war, the other to consolidate a devolved region still racked by sectarianism.

Partition had come to stay. But it was not an outcome that could have been foreseen or desired even a decade earlier. Confrontation over a division within the United Kingdom had led to the prospect of a further division within Ireland. Then, between 1916 and 1925, a series of individual, unco-ordinated actions, cumulatively of unpredictable but major impact, had constructed a 'temporary' Irish partition and then rendered it 'permanent'. It was to defy many subsequent attempts to remove it in the years ahead.

4

SEPARATE WAYS:
1926–38

By the end of 1925 both administrations in Ireland had begun the serious task of building up their infrastructures and implementing their declared policies. The outcome of their Boundary Agreement emphasised for each the paramount need to concentrate on putting its own house in order. Their tasks were separate and urgent. But they were not to be free of association. On the one hand there existed matters of joint concern, while on the other there would be, inevitably, individual decisions from time to time that would have cross-border impact. Already, too, perceptions had developed, the one of the other, fostered by newspaper coverage and influenced by the actions and aspirations of each. Dublin still regarded partition as an aberration and looked to its demise, to the political unification of the island, and to the strengthening of its overall Catholic ethos; Belfast regarded its neighbour with suspicion but retained some hope that it might see the error of its ways and revert to membership of the United Kingdom.

As time passed, however, it would become clear that Dublin had no plans in mind to achieve its unification goal, and that the lack of such a plan was reflected in public apathy towards the northern jurisdiction. Belfast, seeing no sign of a change of heart, but rather, the visible evidence of Catholicisation, would pursue relentlessly a policy of protecting Partition. The regular contacts between governments foreseen in the 1925 Agreement did not take place, evidence, perhaps, of nervousness in the North. The report of a Cabinet Meeting in June 1926 gives a clue:

The Minister of Labour stated that he quite approved of individual Ministers entering a conference with their opposite numbers in the Free State, but that he would strongly disapprove of the two Cabinets doing so, as this would lead to mis-understanding by many in Northern Ireland, who would consider that this was the thin end of the wedge towards a United Ireland. He also pointed out the difference in status of the two Cabinets which also created further difficulty.[1]

So far as practical joint matters were concerned, it was possible in the early years to deal courteously across the border. Railways, especially the company controlling the main line between the two capitals, the Great Northern; contagious diseases, not least those affecting cattle; Public Records; coastal navigation lights; the Post Office and currency were amongst specific items of business, while broader issues included security and trade. But there were also irritants which surfaced frequently, especially those perceived to relate to vital minority interests in each area, the security, employment and fair treatment in general of Catholics in the north and Protestants in the south. General elections, anniversary celebrations and religious festivals, wherever located, tended to generate hostile propaganda, while one or two legal or constitutional disputes, for example the Foyle Fisheries and Carlisle Bridge cases in 1927, contributed to tension in the years up to the first change of government, in 1932. It is not necessary to chronicle every detail of contact during this period, but some examples and their cumulative impact must be observed.

The fact that the 'arch Republican', de Valera, was still in the Free State's political wilderness in 1926 did not fully reassure Craig's government in Belfast: Cosgrave and his Ministers were, after all, pursuing a declared 'stepping stone' policy towards complete independence and republican status. And the evidence of anti-Royal and anti-Commonwealth gestures was not slow in coming. The fine new currency designed by Percy Metcalf for the Free State, which went into circulation in 1926, discarded the King's head; postage stamps had already been subjected to a similar policy. Dublin's failure to get the British

Foreign Office to honour Irish passports which omitted the description 'British Subject', a wrangle which had begun in 1924 and which ran on through the rest of the decade, was less important for its result than for its intention. Dublin, having established its first diplomatic representative in 1924, proceeded to seek its own nationality, its own citizenship, passports and ensign. Although participants in the Imperial Conferences of 1923 and 1926, Irish delegates placed themselves in the van of centripetal rather than centrifugal forces. Their desired direction was not difficult to determine. Then, in 1926, the 'arch Republican' moved out of the wilderness, founding his 'slightly constitutional' Fianna Fail Party in that year and, after the dramatic events of mid-1927 (a general election in June followed by the assassination of Deputy Premier O'Higgins in July and tough new legislation to regulate political activity), he actually took his Party into the Dail. A second general election in the same year, in September, left Fianna Fail breathing down the neck of Cosgrave's Cumann na nGaedheal government. De Valera's stature as republican bogeyman grew apace in Belfast.

Cosgrave's determination to eliminate those aspects of the Treaty deemed to offend national dignity did not diminish. With extremists at his back, indeed, he had an extra argument for winning concessions from London. In 1929 a vigorous attempt was made to remove the Free State citizen's constitutional right of appeal to the Judicial Committee of the Privy Council, and although this was not yet successful, the Dublin government found a method of thwarting any individual attempts to go beyond the decisions of the Irish Supreme Court. This was to enter territory regarded by the tiny Protestant minority as sacrosanct: part of its guarantee of security in this overwhelmingly Catholic state. Increasing censorship by the state, dictated by Catholic conscience, of films from 1923 and publications from 1929, and the effective banning of divorce in 1925 were ominous enough without this abrogation of understandings reached at the time of the Treaty settlement between Protestant and Sinn Fein leaders. They did not pass unnoticed in Belfast.

Belfast, of course, had already proved offensive to a greater degree in regard to minority rights, so far as Dublin was concerned. The turbulent early years had witnessed much sectarian violence and the Catholic community had borne the brunt of the losses of life and employment. The Northern Catholic minority had been outraged, too, at the government's determination to remove what Catholics regarded as a constitutional safeguard, in this instance Proportional Representation, which was abolished for local authority elections in 1922 (taking effect in 1924). The consequent redrawing of electoral boundaries to fit the British first-past-the-post system led to charges of gerrymandering, as one or two sensitive areas, notably the city of Londonderry, had electoral wards adjusted to ensure an overall Unionist majority. Despite strenuous opposition from elected Nationalists, the abolition of PR was extended to the provincial parliament in 1929, though here the result was to have greater impact upon the smaller parties than on the Unionist/Nationalist divide.

The sizeable Catholic minority in Northern Ireland had much more to complain about, however, across a range of political, economic and social areas, and it charged the Unionist authorities with sectarian discrimination in housing, jobs and education, and in security matters, with some substance, if not always to the degree claimed. Before the 1925 Boundary Agreement, Dublin had tried to protect its co-religionists, although the civil war, the shortage of resources and the pressing problems within its own borders had severely limited its practical capacity to do so. After 1925, with the *de facto* recognition of Northern Ireland that the tripartite December Agreement implied, the Northern minority was left to its own devices, directed by Dublin, if asked, to find its salvation through the institutions of the Northern state.

Dublin was concerned with its own sovereignty and wished to go on demonstrating its commitment to its all-island ideal, but apart from isolated and limited displays of sensitivity, lip-service sufficed. The salmon fishery in Lough Foyle, which was owned by the Irish Society, of Londonderry, and which required Belfast legislation in 1927 to ensure its protection from poachers, raised the issue of jurisdiction over territorial waters, something which Dublin claimed. The Irish Society, therefore, should have looked to Dublin for protection, as Dublin's writ by right was deemed to run throughout the waters of this sea lough. Dublin, by now somewhat wary of imperial arbitration, was not confident that in a dispute it could trust the Privy Council to sustain its point of view, and decided not to raise the question at that time. A similar outcome awaited the dispute, which dragged on from 1928 into 1930, over the rebuilding of the Carlisle Bridge, within the city of Londonderry. On the face of it this had nothing to do with the Free State, but the precedent existed for an opening span to permit shipping access to territory upstream in Donegal, and Donegal County Council was keen to keep open a right which had admittedly fallen into desuetude. At the end of the day, however, the Dublin government found that it had no power with which to sustain its point of view.[2]

Meanwhile criticism could be advanced of the Northern government's treatment of its minority, not least in regard to policing and security. The lifting of the threat of border revision in 1925 enabled the immediate disbanding of at least part of the Ulster Special Constabulary. But the force of 'B' Specials that remained, an entirely Protestant force, earned a reputation for partiality in administering justice as well as using up scarce resources that would otherwise have been available for social and medical improvements.

In the field of education, a genuine desire to create a non-denominational primary system, championed by Lord Londonderry as Minister of Education, was frustrated initially by lack of Catholic trust and co-operation. Thereafter, a combination of Protestant clergy and Orange Order initiatives, carefully timed for maximum pressure before elections, in 1925 and 1929, led to the state schools being made to conform to Protestant susceptibilities, while various concessions were also made to assist the separate Catholic school system. This was not entirely satisfactory to the minority, however, as its members contributed to the state schools as tax-payers and had still to make some payments towards the upkeep of their own. These security and educational grievances were exacerbated by resentment at continuing government reliance on the 1922 Special Powers Act, which permitted harsh emergency measures to be implemented on the instruction of the Minister of Home Affairs and which was renewed annually until 1929, then for four years to 1933, and then made permanent. They were exacerbated also by a feeling that too often sectarian discrimination occurred in job allocation, both public and private, and in housing allocation, especially at local authority level. Together they kept alive the resentment of the Catholic population in Northern Ireland and furnished ammunition for criticism from the authorities in Dublin.

The worsening economic depression and severe internal problems in fact ensured that both Irish governments were preoccupied with their own domestic worries in the late twenties and early thirties. In the Free State the added dimension of a threatened breakdown of public order highlighted the approaching general election, due in February 1932. Illegal drilling, intimidation of juries, numerous shootings, the breaking up of party-political meetings by violent attacks (including the prevention by the IRA of an Orange meeting in Cavan, which in turn provoked widespread anti-Catholic reaction in Northern Ireland) together led to a ferocious Public Safety Act being passed by the government in October 1931. This helped to align extremist groups behind de Valera's Fianna Fail Party, already in the ascendant through the government's austerity measures, and contributed to its electoral success in February 1932. De Valera's assumption of power, given the necessary overall majority he needed by the support of the Labour Party when the Dail re-assembled in March 1932, marked a new phase in Dublin–Belfast relations.

So far as Belfast is concerned the change was immediately reflected in correspondence between Prime Minister Craigavon (Craig had been ennobled in 1927) and Sir James O'Grady, then Governor of the Falkland Islands. Writing on 27 June 1932 in reply to a letter from O'Grady, which had alluded to an earlier reflection by Craigavon on the possibility of an Ireland united under one government, perhaps in their lifetime, Craigavon stated unequivocally 'There is now no question. De Valera has forever destroyed any hopes of a united Ireland.'[3]

Unionists would not be interested in union with a Republic. But when in January 1933 de Valera managed to secure an overall Fianna Fail majority, albeit a narrow one, in a further snap general election, some advantage could be perceived from the Unionist perspective. This time it is Lord Londonderry, by now a Junior Minister in the Westminster government, who is writing to Craig, from London:

> My own reaction at present is to find a de Valera government preferable to a Cosgrave government, because in the latter case we on this side would be subject to continual pressure to give way now here, now there, in order to keep Cosgrave popular and in office in the Free State, and as a reward for what he would be sure to regard as his services in having defeated de Valera. In short, as I see it, we are now faced by the more or less open opposition of a de Valera government instead of the somewhat doubtful friendship of a Cosgrave government, whose very existence and goodwill would probably depend entirely upon concessions they could get from us.[4]

From an electoral point of view it was certainly an advantage to have the 'arch Republican' at the helm in Dublin. Nothing could have been better designed to bring the Unionist voters of the North to the polls! There would be little chance of cordial co-operation now. But how much antagonism would be displayed?

The answer was not long in coming, as the new Dublin regime set about asserting its vision of national dignity: a vision that required the destruction of what remained of the 1921 settlement. Unilateral action and confrontation with London was to replace bilateral agreement and a measure of co-operation and understanding. War on two fronts, constitutional and economic, had broken out by July 1932. And if it was the constitutional that in the end was aimed at

Northern Ireland, it was the economic that was destined to bite first.

Eamon de Valera set in motion, in the Dail, legislation to abolish both the Oath of Allegiance to the Sovereign, required of all Dail members, and the right of appeal to the Judicial Committee of the Privy Council, legislation which was not finally enacted until May and November 1933, respectively. By then he had also taken active steps, as a British Cabinet paper observed, to 'minimise as far as possible the importance of the position and the duties of the Governor-General'.[5] But it was in the sphere of economic relations that the change of government first impinged on Anglo-Irish relations, and consequently on the relationship between Belfast and Dublin. For it had been a central plank of Fianna Fail's election platform that the Irish government should no longer continue to forward to London the land annuity payments still being collected from purchasers under the terms of the Land Acts of the late nineteenth and early twentieth centuries.

It was the contention of the new government that these were no longer an obligation, a view that was set out as early as March 1932 in correspondence with J. H. Thomas, the Dominions Secretary. The exchange of letters soon became acrimonious and extended their scope, and on 5 April de Valera took Britain to task for the 'outrage of Partition . . . the alienation of the most sacred part of our national territory, with all the cultural and material loss that this unnatural separation entails'.[6] The rift became public on 11 April, Craigavon being summoned to London hot-foot from a visit to Galloon Island, in Fermanagh, and banner headlines in the following day's *Northern Whig* announced that the 'Free State repudiates settlement of 1921' and 'Ulster must not be sacrificed'. In its defiant leading article the same paper was able to employ a favourite Biblical reference: 'In the eyes of Mr de Valera, Ulster is a Naboth's vineyard, and he and his followers hope that one day the coveted Province will be theirs. But Naboth still says "No"'.[7]

De Valera irritated his British opponents by adding other financial matters which he believed were outstanding, while the British referred pointedly to the settlement reached in 1926 which, in their view, had tidied up all such issues. As half-yearly interest payments became due on 1 July 1932, their non-appearance immediately brought things to a head, and before either realised it, both were engaged in a ruinous economic war. Earlier meetings in June had not prevented it; further negotiations in July and October could not end it; and measure and counter-measure persisted, with some modification in 1935, until the spring of 1938.

These measures took the form of tariffs, a 20 per cent ad valorem duty imposed by the United Kingdom government upon selected Irish imports to recoup the land annuity monies, and a counter-tariff by the Free State government on a selection of imported goods from Britain. These latter duties were to hit Northern Ireland hard and to cause much ill feeling. It gave the Belfast government no delight to see the symbols of monarchy progressively dismantled in the Free State and the guarantees and safeguards cherished by their co-religionists abandoned, but it was in their own pockets that they felt the first results of Fianna Fail policy. As the Northern Minister of Finance, Hugh Pollock, observed, the Free State tariffs were both 'vindictive' and 'unfair' in regard to the distributive and manufacturing sectors in Northern Ireland, especially those of the border towns. Yet, so far as he could detect, they were 'all directed to the weird idea that the loyalty of the border people will be so undermined that they will clamour for admission to the Free State'.[8]

The timing of these events was such that the first encounter between representatives of Belfast and Dublin after the start of economic hostilities was in Ottawa at the important Imperial Economic Conference, convened on 20 July to try to reverse the world slump by increasing inter-Commonwealth trade. There, an uneasy Free State delegation, headed by Sean T. O'Kelly and Sean Lemass, was observed by a semi-official Northern Ireland team consisting of Pollock, Sir Basil Brooke, MP (NI), and Senator McCorkell, loosely attached to the British delegation. This team was active in winning support for their point of view amongst other delegates, and the fact that the Free State was deemed by Britain to be in breach of existing Treaty undertakings meant that no trade agreements were reached with the Irish. Pollock was glad of the opportunity of talking to Prime Minister Baldwin about the specific impact of the trade dispute on Northern Ireland, and recorded with satisfaction that Baldwin 'fully appreciated the arguments (about Free State tariff policies to force us into union with the Free State) and promised that before any permanent form of mutual tariff was settled with the Free State our Government would be consulted. This assurance was freely given, without any pressure on my part.'[9]

Had Cosgrave remained in power he might have made something of the economic opportunity presented by Ottawa. At home his defeat deprived him of another starring role when the International Eucharistic Congress, perhaps the greatest display of Catholic devotion to take place in Ireland thus far, was mounted in Dublin's Phoenix Park in June 1932. It was de Valera who reaped this benefit, but the natural pride felt by Irish Catholics led to a degree of triumphalist rhetoric and to a corresponding increase in Northern Protestant self-assertion. Typically, if regrettably, Northern Catholics travelling back from the celebrations were attacked by hostile mobs in several Ulster towns, and the summer Orange platforms were unusually bitter in their denunciations of Roman bigotry.

Religious tension had been increased the previous year by Cardinal MacCrory who had assured Catholics that the Protestant Church of Ireland was 'not even a part of the Church of Christ', while de Valera had begun openly to stress specifically Catholic priorities.[10] Sectarian statements and claims grew to new heights in 1933, with Basil Brooke being particularly provocative and Craigavon, stout in his defence, prepared to echo Southern identification of the Free State with Catholicism by boasting in his fine new House of Commons (opened at Stormont two years earlier, in 1932), that in contrast 'we are a Protestant Parliament and a Protestant State'.[11] The years 1931 to 1934, when this last statement was made, were perhaps the most notorious for such public expressions, but the years ahead were seldom without minority grievances in one territory or another that caused indignation and sometimes provoked serious outbreaks of disorder.

1934, for example, was distinguished by heartfelt pleas from Donegal Protestant farmers for help from Belfast in what they perceived to be economic persecution by their own authorities. Like many agriculturalists they were suffering from the 'economic war' with Britain, but they also felt peculiarly disadvantaged by the loss of their traditional markets for potatoes and milk in the North. The repeated claims of this community, added to observations that the Protestant population was dwindling in the Free State, down 32 per cent between 1911 and 1926 and still declining; that further safeguards such as the Senate and University Representation were under assault; and that a break with the Commonwealth was feared; that their British citizenship was threatened in 1935; and that specific complaints were voiced of discrimination in employment and in the award of cattle export licences, together meant that in the North the issue of the 'Plight of Loyalists in the Free State'[12] remained a prominent one throughout the decade.

There was no shortage of similar expressions of discrimination against Nationalists in the North, and awareness of this issue by Southern politicians was usually most acute at election times. The January 1933 general election in the Free State was a snap affair, designed to catch the opposition on the wrong foot and to secure an overall Fianna Fail majority, and in the circumstances the North was scarcely an issue. The Northern elections of November 1933 were a different matter, however, with de Valera standing successfully as a Fianna Fail candidate in South Down and his colleague, Eamon Donnelly, with equal success as an abstentionist in West Tyrone. Their triumphs inspired the Northern Government to alter its electoral law the following year, to require all candidates at the time of their nomination to give a commitment that they would take up their seats if elected. The new law also extended from three years to seven the period of residence in the province required of voters. At all costs the Unionists of Ulster must be protected from cross-border 'blow-ins', who would naturally wish to bring down Lord Craigavon's regime!

The 1933 election in the North had been a single-issue occasion: 'Union Jack or Tricolour?'. Apart from Queen's University, only fifteen constituencies were contested, but Craigavon, in a final appeal to the voters in the *Belfast News-letter*, sought an 'emphatic reply' to Dublin where 'ravenous eyes are concentrated upon the Province by those who covet its potentialities in an all-Ireland Parliament and who would rejoice at any sign of weakening on the part of our citizens'. Show the rest of the world, he asked, that 'we still know our own minds!!!' In the same issue, the leading article demanded 'Do Ulster people still value their birthright?' and argued that they must show themselves 'determined that their country shall work out its own destiny as an integral part of the United Kingdom'.[13]

Cross-border recriminations characterised the next general elections, South and North, but in the meantime periodic sectarian violence hit new heights in Belfast in 1935. Each year in the early 1930s there had been trouble: serious anti-Catholic riots in 1931 in Armagh, Lisburn, Portadown and Belfast, following the prevention by the IRA of an Orange meeting in Cavan; not only attacks on attenders at the Eucharistic Congress in 1932, but a nasty flare-up in Belfast that October, resulting in two deaths and many woundings; and in 1933 the murder of a Catholic publican in Belfast's York Street area, where tension remained high throughout the following year. It was in May 1935 that major sectarian riots once more disfigured Belfast, with the Twelfth of July parades being followed by the worst conflict for years, two deaths and thirty-six injuries resulting that night. By 21 July nine people had been killed, scores injured and hundreds driven from their homes, with much damage to property.

Within Northern Ireland charge and counter-charge sought to lay the blame at the door of Unionist and Nationalist alike, but in the context of this study it is the Southern perception of events that is relevant. The *Irish Independent* was not untypical in feeling that the 'dreadful deeds enacted in Belfast must bring shame to every Irishman', and condemned the 'orgy of insane and un-Christian hate', arguing that 'those who by their public utterances have encouraged the sentiments of bitter feud have a heavy responsibility'. As the days passed and headlines such as 'Maddened mob burns Catholic homes' reminded southern readers of the continuing 'shame', a further leader described the 'state of absolute terror' in which Catholics in Belfast were living, and placed Lord Craigavon 'on trial before the whole world'. Sadly, before long, events in the Saorstat itself had to be condemned as 'un-Christian crimes', further headlines noting that 'wanton attacks on Protestants . . . by way of reprisals for the savage persecution of Catholics in Belfast' had occurred in several places.[14] These were unhappy times.

The background to these outbursts in the North was the sustained constitutional and economic conflict between Dublin and London, the more strident republican and irredentist stance of the former contributing, in the Belfast government's view, to the greater militancy of nationalists in the North. By 1937, the time of the next general election in the Free State, de Valera had largely completed his unilateral sweeping aside of what were to him the unacceptable remnants of the 1921 'Treaty'. The time was then ripe for a tidying-up exercise in the form of a new Constitution, and a referendum to adopt this was arranged to coincide with the election date, 1 July. It was the Constitution, with its audacious claims to the whole island, that brought the greatest reaction from Belfast.

There had been little doubt as to the direction that the Free State had been moving. The elimination of the role of the Crown in its Constitution and, indeed, the denial of any interference with its autonomy, had been steadily effected. It had been the Abdication crisis, which had come to a head in December 1936, just five months before, that had given de Valera the opportunity to remove the Crown from his state's internal affairs.[15] Then his emergency legislation had provoked from Belfast, on Saturday 12th, the cynical observation that de Valera 'hopes to establish the Free State as a republic without sacrificing any of the benefits of the British connection'. The *Belfast Newsletter* had observed also the concern shown in the Dail that the legislation might have the effect of 'perpetuating the evil of Partition'; and on this score had felt no doubt about 'its reaction upon the loyalists of Northern Ireland'. And on the following Monday, it had chided the Irish leader for not being able to 'face the hard facts', one such being that 'Ulster people desire nothing more than to be left out of his plans': indeed his actions would have lasting impact on his hopes for eventual Irish unity for (or so the *Newsletter* had opined) he could not have offended Ulster sentiment 'more thoroughly than he did in the Chamber of Deputies on Friday and Saturday'.[16]

Now, in May 1937, he launched a Constitution discernibly if not explicitly republican, recognising the Catholic character of its people and changing the name of the state to Eire. Most provocatively, from a Belfast perspective, Article 2 asserted bluntly

> The national territory consists of the whole island of Ireland, its islands and the territorial seas.

Article 3 recognised reality but nevertheless repeated the implied threat:

> Pending the re-integration of the national territory, and without prejudice to the right of the Parliament and Government established by this Constitution to exercise jurisdiction over the whole of that territory, the laws enacted by that parliament shall have the like area and extent of application as the laws of Saorstát Éireann and the like extra-territorial effect.[17] [For further extracts from the 1937 Consitution see Appendix D.]

The *Belfast Newsletter* typified the Northern response when the Constitution was published on 1 May: 'The claim [on the North] . . . has no reality, whatever the Free State may call itself.'[18] Preoccupied with the coronation of George VI, Ulster Unionists were ill inclined to be diverted by pretensions south of the border. The *Newsletter* was thus equally contemptuous when, on 13 May, republican enthusiasts made their own coronation gesture by blowing up the statue of George II in Dublin: all to be expected, no doubt, but it was necessary to remark upon 'the effrontery of even suggesting that at any time in the future Ulster might consider the question of lying down with such a bedfellow'.[19]

The vision of Ireland that was enshrined in this Constitution owed much to de Valera himself and to current Catholic thinking on social matters: it was rural and romantic, idealistic and non-material, and traditionalist in gender terms, as well as Gaelic and Catholic. Although aspiring to all the island it restricted its operation and its ethos to the 26 counties of the former Free State. It was endorsed by the electorate of that state, though only narrowly, and it came into force on 29 December 1937. 'It ignored the way of life of Ulster Protestants over whom it claimed sovereignty' and its terms helped to consolidate 'a state in the south that could only repel any self-respecting Ulster Protestant', as two scholars in the Irish Republic have recently put it.[20] Fianna Fail was returned to power, but without an overall majority, in the July election. The referendum on the Constitution produced in its favour 685,105 votes, with 526,945 against, a majority of only 158,160. That de Valera could tell his party's annual convention that his Constitution had been passed 'by a majority of the Irish people' can only mean that he defined out of 'the Irish people'[21] the million-strong Protestants of the North. That may have suited them well enough, but there remained the anomaly of the territorial claim.

Fianna Fail recovered its overall majority in a snap election in June 1938, being able to cash in on the successful resolution of Anglo-Irish difficulties. This was effected in a series of agreements, signed on 25 April, which ended the financial arguments, concluded the trade war and returned to Irish control those naval facilities ceded to Britain under the terms of the 1921 'Treaty'. But the nature of these agreements, and indeed their very anticipation, had considerable impact on

Belfast–Dublin relations, while the continuation in power of Fianna Fail ensured that the partitionist mentality so evident in the new Constitution continued to characterise Dublin policy. Romantic slogans embracing the recovery of the 'occupied territory' in Ulster would go on accompanying actions firmly geared to the political and religious ambitions of those in charge in Dail Eireann.

Two aspects of the Anglo-Irish negotiations of 1937–8 were viewed with particular alarm in Belfast: cross-border trade and the very existence of the border itself. It was this latter issue that enabled Craigavon to ensure that his hastily called election of January 1938 was a resounding success. Much discontent had been growing within Unionist ranks at the old and unimaginative government now so long established in office, and a new Progressive Unionist movement was threatening to emerge, under the leadership of W. J. Stewart. Once the press revealed that Dublin–London negotiations were afoot, however, and that de Valera was intending to challenge the continuation of Partition, Craigavon seized his chance. Northern Ireland's general election was fought once more on the single Border issue, internal challenge was overcome, and Unionists, able to view the coming into force of the Eire Constitution on 29 of December as a timely reminder of its unattractiveness, swung solidly behind their long-established Premier.

The trade issue proved more intractable. So far as the British negotiators were concerned, a generous settlement of Irish grievances might lead to closer co-operation in the strained international circumstances of the time; perhaps even to a defence treaty between Dublin and London. There was a lot at stake but to its chagrin, as the negotiations moved into the second week of March, the Chamberlain Cabinet discovered a stubborn Irish refusal to allow the free entry of Northern Irish goods to their territory, a condition deemed by the British to be essential if it was to keep faith with its own promises to Belfast, and if it was to win Belfast's approval for the settlement as a whole. Unemployment in Belfast made it even more imperative there that the status quo ante the economic conflict be restored, but for the Dublin government concessions to Belfast were politically difficult, given its perception of the Northern regime's treatment of its nationalist minority.

By 23 March complete breakdown loomed, as Dublin refused to concede, and it was not until 13 April that the Cabinet in London at last found a compromise by which it would itself offer 'compensation in other directions for the failure to secure preferential treatment from Eire for goods of Northern Irish origin':[22] compensation which took the form of some agricultural subsidies, arrangements to secure relief for some possible future budget deficits, and guarantees in relation to the 1935 Unemployment Insurance Agreement between Belfast and London.

The Northern Ireland view of the settlement as a whole was probably well reflected at the time in the *Belfast Newsletter* when it asserted that Dublin had gained a 'remarkably fine bargain at the expense of the United Kingdom, and particularly perhaps Northern Ireland'.[23] In the context of this account it might be worth adding that the whole tenor of the settlement served to harden relations between North and South. The working out of its terms was soon overtaken by the outbreak of war, but the refusal to accommodate Northern trade can only have served, in the words of a more recent *Irish Times*, 'to cement partition',[24] while the return of the 'Treaty' ports greatly facilitated the neutral stand which Eire chose to adopt in that conflict. And in such circumstances the war itself inevitably added to the reality of the Partition experience.

5

NEUTRAL AND BELLIGERENT: 1938–49

As the international situation deteriorated and war between Britain and Germany became more likely, further exchanges occurred between Dublin and Belfast. The June 1938 election campaign in Eire, with the London Agreements signed and only Partition left as a national grievance, found the ruling Fianna Fail Party strangely quiet about that issue, as de Valera sought to gain political capital from the success of his diplomatic triumphs in April, which he acknowledged to be due in some measure to British 'generosity'. In Belfast it was observed that his 'principal task' now was to end 'Partition'. When this second Dail election within twelve months resulted in a comfortable overall majority, the *Newsletter* could only agree that this was thanks to the British Agreement.[1]

By the autumn, de Valera felt able openly to endorse another initiative towards unity. This time he offered Craig the continuation of his devolved parliament with its powers held from Dublin rather than London, and with guarantees to the nationalist minority in the North that their ordinary rights would be safeguarded. The mature offer, spelled out in the *Evening Standard* of 17 October, resembled a kite flown in an interview given by the Taoiseach to the *New York Times* at the beginning of the year and reported in the *Belfast Newsletter* on 27 January. It had been further rehearsed in discussion with British ministers in late September and early October, for it was de Valera's conviction that they had created the 'mess' of Partition and therefore it was they who had the ultimate responsibility for undoing it. The British refused to contemplate the coercion of the majority in Northern Ireland, however, and the public appeal to Craig evoked no more favourable a response, being vigorously rebuffed in the pages of the *Sunday Despatch* on 23 October. In an interview by the Ulster journalist-peer Lord Donegall, the Northern Premier reiterated his unequivocal position:

> Civil war would follow any attempt to meet Mr de Valera's manifesto on a united Ireland. No Ulster leader could prevent loyalists taking matters into their own hands. . . . [Besides] If Ulster were craven enough to give in it would initiate a process of disintegration at the very heart of the Empire. We have learned in Northern Ireland to place no value whatever on Mr de Valera's promises or even guarantees. They are valueless in Ulster. . . . We in Ulster feel it is time to put a stop to his activities. We are here now to say in no circumstances whatever will we listen to the rattling of the sabre or, for that matter, the cooing of the dove where the integrity of Ulster is concerned.

And in response to the familiar Dublin complaint that the division of Ireland was the fault of others, he roundly asserted:

> The deepest wound that has been inflicted on the Southern Irish was inflicted by themselves owing to their insane insistence on the disintegration of the United Kingdom. They took the initiative. Theirs is the blame.[2]

Craigavon was soon to be forced to seek a closer relationship with de Valera, in the interests of wartime solidarity, but in the meantime there were problems of IRA resurgence in the early months of 1939 to be dealt with, and in the spring a crisis with deep First World War resonances: compulsory conscription into the British forces.

The first of these issues was to cause anxiety in Dublin as well as Belfast and in England, where an IRA campaign of bombings was initiated in January. De Valera was quick to condemn this violent upsurge, accompanied as it was by rather grandiose demands, sent to Berlin and Rome as well as London, for Britain to quit Ireland. His own policy was to pursue unity peacefully, but it was not without some justice that the Belfast regime pointed to his irredentist rhetoric as part of the explanation as to why young men were prepared to take up arms.[3] In a speech in Manchester, Basil Brooke, then Northern Ireland's Minister of Agriculture, contemptuously compared de Valera's claims with those of Hitler upon Czechoslovakia's Sudetenland.[4] In the atmosphere created by Dublin's unity drive it was not surprising that gullible and lonely Irish workers in England, and disenchanted Northern Irish nationalists, for that matter, could be persuaded to adopt a more active and belligerent stance.

The threat of conscription was to produce a series of crises of a rather different order. De Valera was haunted by the memory of Redmond's generous espousal of the call to arms in August 1914, and was fully aware of the emotional impact of the conscription issue as it had come to a head in the tense spring months of 1918. Thus, when the United Kingdom's Compulsory Military Training Bill was introduced on 26 April 1939, containing a clause to permit it to be extended to Northern Ireland, an extension immediately endorsed by Craig, de Valera did not hesitate to cancel an arranged trip to New York to lead the campaign of nationalist opposition. The Irish hierarchy, headed by Cardinal MacRory, firmly backed a campaign based on the moral indefensibility of the recruitment of one people into the army of another. Craig was equally determined that Northern Ireland should be treated as any other part of the United Kingdom, and that it should bear its share of the common burden. He was aware that there could be problems of implementation: that some might flee across the border to avoid recruitment; that resistance might be offered in Nationalist areas; that other nationalists might take the military training before absconding; that the jobs of those recruited might be filled by incomers from Eire, who would cause present resentment and future trouble. But he was nevertheless clear where the province's duty lay and he was deeply chagrined when, after being called to London on 2 May to give his views to Chamberlain, he was asked to be helpful and not press for conscription in Northern Ireland. The British newspapers had already expressed their fear of unrest should conscription be attempted and as Lady Craig was to record in her diary:

The British Government were frightened of the issue being complicated by de Valera kicking up a dust, though Ulster affairs have *nothing* to do with him. American opinion, as ever, had to be considered too. The military authorities in Belfast also advised against it, on account of the trouble that might arise on the Falls Road when forcibly going to enlist people.[5]

Craig felt humiliated, especially when taunted in his own House of Commons that de Valera seemed to carry more weight with the British government than he did.[6] De Valera was gratified, and one of his supporters claimed at his party's annual convention in December that the achievement had had a 'tremendous influence in securing respect in the North for the Government of Eire. The people of the North were grateful to the Government of the South for having saved their sons from the slaughter of the war.'[7] But the issue was not so simple as that! For by then the war had broken out and Eire's aspiration to adopt neutrality had been implemented. For the two jurisdictions in Ireland there had been a new and more real parting of the ways.

The conscription issue was to complicate relations between Belfast and Dublin on two further occasions in the early years of the war. In May 1940, soon after he had replaced Chamberlain as Prime Minister, Churchill called Craigavon to London where the Ulster leader once more requested its application and was once more rebuffed. The main issue at the time was the need for a local defence force, and although this, the Home Guard as it became, was acceptable to nationalist sentiment, in the event Northern Ireland's version was implemented on strictly traditional lines through recruitment from the Special Constabulary.

More serious, because more public, was the effort made by the government of J. M. Andrews in the aftermath of the Belfast blitz, which had so devastated the city in April and May 1941. Although Andrews had brought up the conscription issue as early as 4 April, before the first bombings, the subsequent British request, in the form of a telegram enquiry from Home Secretary Morrison on 20 May, came at a time when it was thought the public mood in Northern Ireland would be responsive to the idea, now that so much suffering had been experienced at German hands. The Belfast Cabinet returned an immediate and positive reply to make clear that it was 'emphatically of the opinion that conscription should be applied to Northern Ireland'.[8]

Then, on 22 May, Churchill confided to the Commons that he was thinking of so extending conscription, only to release once more an explosion of nationalist hostility to the idea throughout Ireland. De Valera's views were passed to the London government by High Commissioner Dulanty, and it is clear that he felt deeply uneasy that the unrest such a move would release might enhance IRA standing and even provoke a German invasion. The Inspector General of the RUC, Lt Col. Charles Wickham, was far more aware of the trouble to be expected than were his political masters and his report on the situation to Home Secretary Morrison, along with continuous evidence from Dublin, Belfast and America, helped to convince London to change its mind. It was Churchill himself who had to eat his words, admitting to the House on 27 May, 'we have come to the conclusion that at the present time . . . it would be more trouble than it is worth to enforce such a policy'.[9]

The outbreak of war on 3 September 1939 and the distinction drawn between neutral Eire and Northern Ireland, which remained an integral part of the belligerent United Kingdom, led to pressures other than those caused by conscription, and the *Annual Register* records that 'there was a good deal of controversy in the Northern Parliament as to the attitude of the North to the South'.[10]

Even so, by early June 1940, with the war proceeding disastrously, the fall of France imminent and with Churchill newly installed in No. 10 Downing St, it looked as though some drastic measure might be necessary to protect Britain's flank by bringing Eire into the war. Neville Chamberlain, now Lord President of the Council, summoned Craig to London and on 5 June urged him to seek some arrangement with de Valera that might induce the Irish leader to 'take more effective measures for the defence of the country against German invasion'.[11] Thus began a hectic sequence of events that culminated a month later in de Valera rejecting a British offer of Irish unity in return for defence co-operation and the opening of Irish facilities to British forces.

Not that it was Craig who set the hectic pace. Rather it was the absence of action from him in the following week that helped move Chamberlain first to seek a meeting with the two Irishmen in London, and then, failing that, to despatch Malcolm MacDonald, Churchill's Minister of Health, on 17 June to Dublin to urge upon de Valera the urgent need for action. In all, MacDonald made three trips to the Irish capital, the original defence co-operation suggestion expanding into an offer of unity, providing Belfast agreed (Craig, meanwhile, remaining in the dark as to these developments). On 26 June, the day that MacDonald was making definite proposals to de Valera, Chamberlain communicated these also to Craig by letter, causing the Ulster leader 'profound shock' and drawing from him a charge of 'treachery'.[12]

The proposals were not to the liking of the Irish Cabinet, however, and even in expanded form were formally rejected by letter, handed to Chamberlain by Dulanty on 5 July.[13] By then Craig had made a public offer of defence co-operation with de Valera, in the interests of survival, but on condition that his opposite number in Dublin expelled Axis representatives from that city, stood by the Empire and undertook not to raise any constitutional issues. This, too, lacked attraction for de Valera and once he had made his rejection clear Craig swore that such an offer 'will not be raised by me again'.[14]

Throughout these negotiations British ministers had repeatedly stressed that if the two parts of Ireland joined together in comradely struggle against the common foe then the implications for eventual unity would be enormous, whereas, if they found themselves in different camps, the one involved, the other neutral, then unity would be postponed indefinitely. The Irish Premier was reluctant to jeopardise his concept of independence, however, and continued to seek unity in neutrality, something that was unacceptable to Britain and anathema to the Northern Irish authorities. He refused to co-operate and, while Irish pride was undoubtedly enhanced by successful pursuit of neutrality through years of difficulty, it was a pride very different from that taken by the bulk of citizens in Northern Ireland through partnership in a just international cause eventually crowned by Allied victory.

Craig's death in November 1940 ensured that the finality of his offer was literally so. It also drew an era to an end: an era of personal antagonism, intransigence and mutual incomprehension between two men personifying the historical poles of Irish experience. Time would tell whether new leaders would appear with alternative approaches and more winning ways. In the short term, however, there was a war to be won, and an Emergency to be survived.

The two issues came momentarily together in April 1941 when the worst fears of a largely unprotected Belfast were realised and the German Luftwaffe pounded the city with one of the most intensive air-raids of the war. On Easter Tuesday night, 15/16 April, after experiencing a somewhat cursory initial raid on its docks the previous week on 7/8th, Belfast suffered a full-scale blitz of terrifying dimension which killed almost seven hundred people (nearly four hundred of them women and children), and destroyed and damaged many homes as well as strategic and war-production facilities. At the height of the destruction, in the early hours of 16 April, when the raid was still in progress and when its scale and effectiveness had revealed Belfast's resources to be 'generally very good, but completely inadequate to the task which faced them',[15] a request was sent to Dublin for fire-fighting assistance.

It was immediately forthcoming, some seventy men and thirteen appliances arriving from Dublin, Dun Laoghaire, Drogheda and Dundalk later that morning. In a public statement made in Castlebar on Saturday 19 April, Mr de Valera, who had authorised this assistance, offered his sympathy and such aid as he could give to those in distress: they were, after all, he told his audience, 'our people', and he was sure that 'were the circumstances reversed they would also give us their help wholeheartedly'.[16] Quietly, on the same day, W. T. Cosgrave, on behalf of his own family and his colleagues, wrote to Prime Minister Andrews of his 'respectful, sorrowful sympathy with the Government and people of Northern Ireland in their loss and suffering'. He asked Andrews not to bother replying, but was sent a 'deeply touched' acknowledgement two days later. Indeed the Belfast authorities were genuinely grateful for the help extended to them, by public bodies, by the Irish Red Cross, by the railway services and by the generosity of many private individuals in Eire who sent donations or who accommodated refugees.[17]

The bond of gratitude diminished somewhat in the ensuing differences over conscription, when once again it seemed that Unionist advice was being ignored in favour of that from Dublin. The true colours of the Dublin regime were deemed to have reappeared soon enough when, in the immediate aftermath of Pearl Harbor and the entry of the United States into the war, Churchill sent his final plea to de Valera: 'Now is your chance. Now or never. A nation once again.'[18] This was a return to the appeal of solidarity in the fight against Nazism, an invitation to abandon neutrality and win comradely hearts. But even interpreted as an invitation to do a deal on Partition it was not acceptable to de Valera. Talks between him and Dominions Secretary Lord Cranborne on 17 December clarified matters but there was to be no change. 'In existing circumstances', Cranborne reported of de Valera, 'with the Partition problem as an open sore, any attempt to bring a United Ireland into the war on our side would be doomed to failure.' 'From this position', he added, 'I could not budge him.'[19]

And the full and public return to old attitudes was quickly completed upon the arrival shortly afterwards, on 26 January 1942, of the first batch of American troops upon Northern Irish soil. All in all, more than 100,000 American servicemen were to assemble in the Province before the Allied invasion of the Continent was begun in 1944; not only soldiers and airmen but also sailors, who manned the naval base quickly established at Londonderry. But this first batch offended de Valera's dignity, for his government 'had not been consulted either by the British Government or the American Government', and it was at odds with his view of the national territory. So he issued a statement reiterating his claim to 'supreme jurisdiction'[20] over the whole island, intensely annoying Unionists, who were perhaps equally outraged by Cardinal MacRory later in the year, inferring an American invasion when he complained at witnessing his own 'corner of [his] country overrun by British and United States soldiers against the will of the nation'.[21] North–South relations had returned to normal.

And for the rest of the war this is largely how they remained. It has been shown convincingly that Irish neutrality always operated in a way friendly towards Britain, whose forces and trading resources helped sustain the Irish people during the period, and that this neutrality became more benevolent over time, especially after America's entry on the side of the Allies. After the early exchanges of 1942, pressure was mounted by both Washington and London upon Dublin from time to time, and contacts at top level were discouraged. In mid-March 1942 formal statements of position were made by de Valera and Andrews, the traditional St Patrick's Day broadcast by the Taoiseach sparking both a sharp rejoinder from the Ulster Premier, and a *Belfast Newsletter* leading article on Monday 19 March entitled 'The Dublin Ostrich'.

De Valera spoke of the 'unnatural dismemberment' of his country standing in the way of its 'most effective defence. . . a unified defence organised by the Irish people themselves'. His argument got short shrift from Andrews who pointed out that a proper unified defence would be

possible if Eire is prepared to take its share in the war against the Axis Powers and to accept all the implications of belligerency. Otherwise it is impossible. For Northern Ireland there can be no neutrality in this war; the very idea is abhorrent, seeing that such grave issues are at stake. . . . Mr de Valera's broadcast is just another smoke screen intended to conceal his foolish policy of standing apart from the struggle, on the outcome of which the fate of Eire, no less than the British Empire and all the allied nations, depends.[22]

There the matter rested, so far as Andrews was concerned, for on 30 April 1943 he reluctantly bowed to discontent amongst his own backbenchers at his government's lack-lustre performance and resigned, Sir Basil Brooke assuming office the following day. The tribute paid by Churchill to Andrews on 9 May, on his appointment as a Companion of Honour, emphasised not only his record of devotion to the Union and to the war effort, but also the fact that during his Premiership 'the bonds of affection between Britain and the people of Northern Ireland have been tempered by fire and are now, I firmly believe, unbreakable'.[23] In July, after a brief visit to the province, Herbert Morrison added his own praise of Northern Ireland, contrasting its war commitment to Eire's neutrality and emphasising its 'positive and courageous loyalty to the cause of freedom'.[24]

In 1944 both Irish regimes were beginning to look forward to peace, but while Belfast had endorsed the vision of William Beveridge and had been assured of full and equal welfare treatment within the United Kingdom, de Valera in July and his party in October focused their minds on the single remaining objective of ending the 'iniquity' of Partition. And in 1945, with the war close to its conclusion, a campaign was begun in earnest in July to achieve that end: a campaign dismissed by Brooke, who found the Irish Border a perfectly natural and understandable phenomenon:

> The Border is merely an outward sign of that which is in our heads and in our hearts. We have no doubt as to our constitutional position. We do not have to look at a dictionary to see what our Constitution means. That Constitution is in our hearts.
>
> Those politicians who talk about the iniquity of the Border should realise that what we have here in Northern Ireland is, in fact, a miniature of what exists in other parts of the world . . . boundary divisions which have arrived and which have been caused by differences in mind and heart.[25]

The facts of wartime experience had been so different on both sides of the border. Both peoples had suffered hardships: rationing of many foodstuffs from the beginning in the North and acute shortages of clothing materials, fuel and many commodities throughout the island. The North had also suffered a devastating blitz but its citizens had experienced too the excitements of war campaigns that turned from anticipated defeat to confidence in victory as the tide of Axis advance was turned and, from North Africa to Europe and into Asia, increasing numbers of peoples were liberated from the grip of racist fascism.

And their economy had been transformed. Unemployment, high at the beginning of hostilities, had taken more than a year to fall to an insignificant level, but thereafter, with dramatic increases in every aspect of agriculture, except pig production, which needed imported supplements, and huge expansion in traditional industries, textiles, shipping and aircraft, munitions and engineering, as well as quarrying and construction, and the dramatic development of many new products, bringing wages and savings and the satisfaction of a major contribution to the war effort, the province had been rejuvenated. Furthermore, the shift from war aims to peace planning increasingly held out the hope of further transformation, a growth in social services and welfare, educational opportunity, and an increase in health provision and in communications to bring this backward part of the kingdom up to the new standards deemed appropriate to all: due reward for sacrifice and endeavour throughout the long and costly years of war.

In Eire, the requirements of censorship hid much of this adventure from the people, while the relatively isolated position of this island neutral meant that there were shortages, and unemployment and emigration mounted so that hardships were widespread and protracted. Tea, sugar and fuel were rationed on the outbreak of war; bread and clothing were added in 1942, and gas and electricity soon after. Petrol for private motoring disappeared in 1942, along with household coal, while over-used and resource-starved railway stock deteriorated, along with much industrial and engineering plant. The lack of raw materials reduced job opportunities and increased demands on lowered social benefits.

Jobs were to be found in England, and in the British forces, but, unlike in the First World War, no great opportunity for agricultural profits was available. Here the run-down nature of Irish farms, a foot and mouth epidemic early on, controlled British prices and an absence of fertilisers and imported feeding stuffs played their part. Sterling assets were built up to a degree, but survival was the extent of the Irish economic achievement and stagnation and introspection generally characterised these war years.

Both parts of Ireland survived, then, but in their separate ways, pursuing their different goals, and the border between them took on a new solidity and endurance, physically and psychologically. This development was taken further by events immediately following the war, as Eire, slow to drag itself from economic depression and backwardness, nevertheless adopted the new title of Republic of Ireland and departed from the Commonwealth association, while Northern Ireland experienced a wholesale physical transformation as part of a United Kingdom-wide welfare state, and at the same time fought off a vigorous Dublin-led anti-Partition campaign.

Churchill, in the hour of Germany's defeat, set the tone of appreciation felt by Britain for the war effort of Northern Ireland, emphasising 'its loyalty and friendship'. The following month his words were more measured as he sought to give the Northern Premier support on the eve of the province's general election. After assuring Brooke of his own best wishes and the 'best wishes and the gratitude of the British race in every corner of the globe', he wrote:

> The stand of the Government and people of Northern Ireland for the unity of the British Empire and Commonwealth and for the great cause of freedom for which we all risked our survival will never be forgotten by Great Britain. It enabled the British nation to live and to use its mighty power in the world crusade without coming into physical collision with Mr de Valera's Government and thus prevented a new agonising breach between us and Southern Ireland. A strong, loyal Ulster will always be vital to the security and well-being of our whole Empire and Commonwealth.[26]

But Churchill's defeat at the British general election held on 5 July 1945 in some ways cast a cloud over the future. In one sense it was encouraging that the party with the firmest commitment to the Beveridge vision had won power. Northern Ireland could look forward to considerable investment as the five evils of want, unemployment, ill-health, ignorance and squalor were rooted out and their opposites fostered. On the other hand, this investment might now be made in a more socialistic manner than would appeal to conservative Unionists; and besides, Labour had a traditional weakness for Irish unity and contained within its parliamentary representatives a grouping specifically calling itself 'The Friends of Ireland'.

The Brookeborough government, returned to power though not without some criticisms of its war record by the electorate, on 14 June 1945, felt obliged to weigh these conflicting prospects once Labour took office. The alternatives of moving towards dominion status or in a contrary direction into full integration into Westminster through ending devolved government were examined carefully over the next twelve months. By then the unacceptable cost of moving outside the United Kingdom had been ascertained and the measure of the Attlee Cabinet's support for Northern Ireland's position established. Things were working out well and, despite reverberations of discontent with socialistic legislation during the following couple of years, the overall gains from the present relationship meant that it was never seriously challenged. And when the moment of truth arrived at Easter 1949 with the Republic of Ireland's withdrawal from the Commonwealth, the rapport established between Belfast and London paid off handsomely.

Eire emerged from the war experience but slowly. Rationing and shortages (especially of fuel, which had a knock-on effect upon industry) persisted, exacerbated by harsh winters, a recovering world little prepared to favour those who had stood aside from the conflict, and a laudable self-denying effort to assist war-ravaged peoples with food aid. Wartime planning, which envisaged a greater degree of state intervention to ensure full employment seemed, for a time anyway, to lose its way. Trade union discontent grew. Church and state quarrelled on social issues. Emigration continued.[27] One political catch-cry remained constant, however: the need to end Partition.

The advent of Labour to power in Britain, alarming at first to unionists, had been of equal encouragement to nationalists, who sought to capitalise on their good fortune by founding in November 1945 an Anti-Partition League. An active role in the Stormont parliament was also called for as a succession of bills was introduced to implement wide-ranging education, health and social policies, all of potential benefit to the nationalist community but some with perceived religious dangers. There were several centres of focus therefore, in Dublin and overseas, and in Northern Ireland itself, for the push towards Irish unity, and numerous issues upon which to sharpen debate.

Traditional Unionist views persisted however, and in October 1946 former Premier J. M. Andrews offered a not untypical response to the invigorated nationalist opposition:

> they have failed completely to-day to tell us how socially, industrially, agriculturally, or in any other way, Northern Ireland would benefit by joining an all-Ireland republic. In my opinion she would wither and decline, and all classes in our community would suffer to a deplorable degree.

And he added, for good measure, 'No one, in my opinion has done so much to divide Ireland, both in years of peace and war, as Mr de Valera.' His own solution was to:

> 'Let well enough alone'. I hope that the rulers of Eire will be willing, and if they are willing, there is no reason why, under our two Parliaments, we should not live side by side as friends and neighbours, each governing its own people in accordance with their views, as democratically expressed at election times. Surely this is freedom and justice which no one can deny.[28]

If this parliamentary performance lacked a certain polish, it was none the less sincere. And its reference to an all-Ireland republic harked back to a speech by the Irish leader in Dail Eireann, on 17 July 1945. Goaded on 11 July by Deputy James Dillon to state precisely the nature of Ireland's constitutional position, he had given an assurance that Eire was indeed 'a republic'. Then on 17 July he had set out to prove this contention, bringing to his aid a formidable array of dictionaries[29] (this speech also being the inspiration for Brookeborough's remarks quoted above).

Andrews also had in mind, perhaps, the steady direction taken by Dail governments since 1922: a direction consistently unappealing to Protestant Unionists. It was natural enough for an overwhelmingly Catholic people to give expression to its religion, and in this process Mr de Valera had outstripped his rival, as John Whyte has recorded:

> Mr Cosgrave refused to legalise divorce; Mr de Valera made it unconstitutional. Mr Cosgrave's government regulated films and books; Mr de Valera's regulated dance halls. Mr Cosgrave's government forbade propaganda for the use of contraceptives; Mr de Valera's banned their sale or import.[30]

Furthermore, though Irish unity was Mr de Valera's declared goal, it was not to be achieved at any price. As he declared in Seanad Eireann in February 1939 in response to a rare request to take the 'sentiments and interests' of the Northern Unionists into more serious consideration: 'I would not tomorrow, for the sake of a united Ireland, give up the policy of trying to make this a really Irish Ireland', and he went on to make clear that the preservation of the Irish language and of the power to determine the form of native government and that government's relations with other nations should not be surrendered 'in advance to anybody or for any consideration . . . even the consideration of a united Ireland'.[31] Already in his Constitution he had given priority to just these considerations. Soon his political opponents would go further, declare Ireland a Republic in name as well as spirit, and withdraw it from that Commonwealth Association by which Northern Unionists set such store.

The events leading to the creation of the first Inter-Party government in Eire are fascinating but lie outside this narrative. They were a response to sixteen unbroken years of Fianna Fail rule and to the uncomfortable circumstances of post-war shortage and disillusion referred to above. De Valera, with eighteen months of his mandate still to run, called a snap election for 4 February 1948. His aim was to ditch the new Clann na Poblachta Party, founded in July 1946 and led by Sean MacBride, which had begun to capture the public imagination. With hitherto militant roots it sought now the achievement of a united Irish republic by political means and embodied much current Catholic social teaching in its programme. It had already won two by-election victories and, in confident mood, it proved able to put some ninety candidates into the general election field.

In the event Valera's political judgement appeared sound. His own party held its vote, increased its seats by one, to 67, and remained confident, as the only large party, of continuing in office. Clann na Poblachta, in contrast, won only ten seats. Yet so strong was the urge to 'Put Fianna Fail out' that the most unlikely conjunction of disparate groups came together after the election to form an alternative government, under the Premiership of John A. Costello, and with McBride in charge of Foreign Affairs. It was this coalition that took the decision to make the final break from the Commonwealth and adopt a new title for the state.

Controversy still surrounds the timing and announcement of this decision, made public by Costello in Ottawa on 7 September 1948, but it is its subsequent impact on North–South relations that concerns us here. Back in Dublin, Costello explained his purpose as that of taking the gun out of Irish politics and clearing up once and for all the international position of the state. He was not unaware that his decision would be ill received in Belfast but felt that it would make no practical difference in this regard, and he was bitter in the Dail in his criticism of the negative attitude of Belfast where friendly overtures by this Government or any Government in this part of the country to the Northern Ireland Government would still be opposed by the same cascade of scorn and derision as had been directed by the northern ruling classes towards every constructive suggestion from Irish leaders for the ending of Partition.[32]

Basil Brooke's response was forthright, in the Stormont parliament six days later:

Mr Costello must have known that talk about the intractable ruling classes in Northern Ireland was just so much rubbish. The men and women who are rulers in this country are the ordinary men and women in the street, the workers in the factories, on the farms and in business. . . . To say the ruling classes are keeping the two apart is nonsense.

He proceeded to argue that if a wooer wished to make a good impression then it behoved that person to 'make a decent approach', but 'what the Free State is after is the rape of Ulster; it is not marriage'. His conclusion was that 'the only solution to this very difficult situation which exists in Ireland as a whole, is two Governments'.[33]

Talks took place between Irish and British ministers and also Commonwealth leaders, during October and November 1948, to determine the future relationships between the Irish Republic, planned to be inaugurated at Easter 1949, and the members of the Commonwealth Association, including Britain. The outcome recognised the long historical links between these countries, most with substantial Irish immigrant communities, and old trading and citizenship privileges were retained. Reassurances were freely given to Northern Unionists that their position within the United Kingdom would remain unaffected, but there was no enthusiasm there at the continuing enjoyment by their Irish neighbours of former Commonwealth benefits. In London it could wittily be remarked of the transformation of the hitherto reluctant Dominion that, while it had before agreed 'to be excluded inside the Commonwealth' it was now to be 'included outside the Commonwealth',[34] but resentment simmered in Belfast.

Brooke took his opportunity. On 23 January 1949 he announced a general election.

The build-up of the anti-Partition thrust had been substantial. Once out of office in 1948, Mr de Valera had embarked on an energetic campaign, in America and Australia as well as at home, on the 'Partition must go' slogan, and this had been mirrored by MacBride at every international opportunity. It would seem that the international community had grown irritated by these tactics, but there is little doubt that when the policy led to all-Party endorsement at a Conference at Dublin's Mansion House, on 27 January, and this was followed by an authorised church-gate collection on Sunday 30th, which raised the substantial sum of £46,000 to assist the election of Nationalist candidates in the North, Unionists were handed the single-issue focus that they needed for electoral success. Their ranks closed behind Brooke and he won a substantial victory at the polls on 10 February.

Further success was at hand. Legislation was required in Britain to effect the decisions reached on the Republic's relationships and also to reinforce the assurances given to Northern Ireland. It was when the terms of Westminster's Ireland Bill were announced, on 3 May, that Dublin at last realised the impact of its action and Belfast the place it had lately won in British esteem (see Appendix E).

Contained within the arrangements set out in the bill was a clause almost certainly agreed between Brooke and Attlee in January, and withheld from Dublin until the last minute:[35]

> It is hereby declared that Northern Ireland remains part of His Majesty's dominions and of the United Kingdom and it is hereby affirmed that in no event will Northern Ireland or any part thereof cease to be part of His Majesty's dominions and of the United Kingdom without the consent of the parliament of Northern Ireland.[36]

This was bitterly resented in Dublin as an unwarranted commitment to the status quo, a gratuitous insult to a people partitioned against its will by superior force. But that is not how things looked to the authorities in Belfast or London, or even to dispassionate foreign observers. The Northern government took satisfaction at the copper fastening of its security within the United Kingdom. Prime Minister Attlee in London was low-key but firm, and perceptive too as to the underlying priorities in Dublin. In the Commons on 11 May he stated: 'I had to conclude that the government of Eire considered the cutting of the last tie which united Eire to the British Commonwealth was a more important objective of policy than ending partition.'[37] His Home Secretary, Morrison, reminded the Commons that the United Kingdom government was not the initiator of what had happened, but was simply reacting to an Irish initiative and doing so with exemplary generosity.

The representatives of France in London and Dublin, neutrals in the matter, one must assume, passed their respective judgements. Ambassador Massigli in the former, in a coded despatch on 7 May, wrote that 'one is tempted to think that if the problem of Irish unity is now practically insoluble, then a good part of the blame lies with Dublin',[38] adding a week later that it was not London but Dublin itself 'which had tightened the shackles which bind Ireland'.[39] In Dublin, for his part, Minister Ostrorog had reflected on 6 May on the British guarantee:

> By accepting, on the one hand, the Irish statute of independence gracefully, and by consolidating, on the other hand, the regime established in 1920 for the Six Counties of the North, the British Government undoubtedly has tried to give justice to each. Different attitudes can be taken to this difficult event, each one representing considerable drawbacks. The future will say if the English choice has been wise.[40]

'The achievement of sovereignty' had once again, as it had done consistently since 1921, taken precedence over 'the aspiration to unity' as Professor Fanning has observed,[41] a point earlier made by Garret FitzGerald, reviewing fifty years of partition in July 1971. After surveying Dublin's social and economic policies of the interwar and war years the future Taoiseach pointed 'the paradox that it was the south which, after 1921, chose to grow apart from the north, and thus to copper fasten partition'.[42] Dublin had taken this further step, careless, it appears, of Northern Unionist reaction, and underestimating the degree to which wartime comradeship had cemented the Belfast–London relationship. London had responded and the gap between the two parts of Ireland was left as wide, if not wider, than ever. Professor Fanning had one further point to make in the context of the time, one that underpinned so much of what Northern Unionism was about. The values of independent Ireland, he commented, had also expressed themselves consistently in terms exclusive of Irish Protestant opinion, both north and south of the border. And he noted that it was with a further dramatic expression of just those values that the new decade was about to open.[43]

6

NEIGHBOURS OF A KIND:
1950–72

Although the 1950s were destined to widen dramatically the differences between the two Irish jurisdictions, and to produce contrasting levels of economic and social performance, they dawned on a misleadingly similar note throughout the island, with both regimes anticipating improved conditions for their people.

The new Republic had witnessed something of a post-war consumer boom, as pent-up wartime demand was met. At the same time capital development increased, industry and tourism expanded and the 1951 census recorded a modest addition of 5,000 to the population, marking an end to decades of decline. A new government had offered new hope and by the autumn of 1950 it seemed about to address some of the welfare issues that were being so energetically tackled in the North as part of the United Kingdom's response to the Beveridge Report.

In its 1947 Health Act, Fianna Fail had begun this process by taking the powers necessary to initiate changes in maternity provision, though nothing had been achieved in this regard by the time that government fell. Now Costello's Minister for Health, Noel Browne, who had already overseen remarkable success in the struggle to eliminate tuberculosis, proposed to bring in a radical scheme of state-funded support. Details of his 'Free Mother and Child Welfare Service', as the *Sunday Independent* described it, first appeared in that paper's scoop of 10 September 1950. By the following March, however, it became clear that Archbishop McQuaid of Dublin and his episcopal colleagues were not happy with a measure deemed by them to conflict with Catholic teaching. The hierarchy, it seems, had grown increasingly anxious at the steady growth in state power and had decided to draw the line at a measure believed to undermine individual responsibility, the rights of the family and in this instance also the rights of the church, especially in relation to such sensitive areas of 'Faith and Morals' as sexual relationships, sex and health education, and even, perhaps, birth limitation and family planning.

A crisis in Church–State relations loomed and the fact that it was resolved by the total capitulation of the government became all too clear when, first, Browne resigned on 11 April and then, secondly, details became public when he chose to publish his reasons and also the correspondence that had been exchanged between the conflicting parties. Bitter Dail debates added to the publicity and the split occasioned in Clann na Poblachta and in the Inter-Party government proved fatal to both. In a general election on 30 May, forced by further defections and the loss of the government's majority, the Clann was reduced to two members and the government was put out of office. To Unionists in the North the whole affair was but proof of their long-held conviction: Home Rule was Rome Rule.[1]

But if the religious incompatibilities of the two peoples of Ireland seemed to have been reinforced by this affair, it was their contrasting economic and social circumstances that characterised the rest of the decade. The high initial hopes of the Republic turned to ashes as stagnation and successive economic crises followed, most notably in 1952 and 1956, while emigration, that barometer of national economic health, once more indicted Inter-Party and Fianna Fail regimes alike. Although Costello was given a second opportunity between 1954 and 1957 the awful haemorrhage of the departing young saw an estimated population loss since the foundation of the state of over 400,000 by the time of the 1961 census. That exercise revealed also that the population then stood some 5 per cent below the figure at independence in 1922. It was a bitter commentary, especially when the post-war progress of those Irish citizens still within the British state was observed. To be fair, steps had already been taken that would lead to results in the sixties, but the contrast of the fifties was stark.

In Northern Ireland, the Brooke government, having assured itself of the advantages of the status quo, initially expressed in continued agricultural subsidies and in the favour of the Labour Ministry, soon began to benefit also from the unfolding provisions of the Welfare State.

Services and taxation parity between Northern Ireland and the rest of the United Kingdom was formally agreed during 1946, so that when the British National Insurance scheme came into force in 1948 it applied equally throughout the realm (incorporating the National Insurance Act (NI), 1946, to which was added further supplemenatry legislation in the early 1950s). Also in 1948 were enacted similar measures covering national assistance, family allowances, non-contributory pensions and the health service. Already, public health administration had been overhauled and tuberculosis attacked along lines akin to those to be adopted by Browne in the Republic. In 1949 welfare services were further extended to provide residential accommodation for the needy, and specialist services for the deaf, blind and other handicapped persons.

In education, the British legislation of 1944 was mirrored in the province in 1947 in an Act that was to have the most far-reaching implications for all Northern Irish citizens, making available to both communities much better secondary schooling, free to those academically qualified, and open access through scholarships to third-level institutions. Better housing, incentives to industry and improvements to the communications infrastructure provided a further lift to the material well-being of all in the province.

Unemployment was to persist in these years, at a rate that varied from 6 per cent to 10 per cent, and the government had to work hard merely to stand still, as the decline of traditional staples, agriculture, ship and linen manufactory, and engineering, counterbalanced success in attracting new employment. But whether employed or unemployed, those resident in Northern Ireland were able, through greatly enhanced material circumstances, including higher unemployment benefit, to enjoy, perhaps for the first time, a markedly better standard of living than their counterparts in the Republic. While both parts of Ireland lagged behind British levels, the period of the war and the decade thereafter saw Northern citizens some 20 per cent better off than those in the rest of the island.[2] Increasingly the government in Dublin was forced to devote its whole attention to its immediate domestic problems; while in the North, nationalists found themselves unable to derive much comfort from the Republic's unsatisfactory performance and began seriously to question the wisdom of seeking unity with it.

But if they could count their material blessings with increasing ease and frequency, Northern nationalists could find no comparable blessings in the political sphere. Even as the welfare state began to take beneficent shape, Unionist determination to protect the province from southern infilt-ration, to ensure that ex-servicemen were able to resume their jobs, and to preserve the interests of property-owners in local government – all measures directly related to the delicate balance of Unionist control – had antagonised nationalist opinion. Schooling and hospital disagreements had added to the nationalist conviction that there was no chance for them of equal justice from their Unionist governors unless the political mould could be broken. The inflexibility of Unionist institutions and attitudes was to bring this issue to a head in the 1960s. It was in the 1950s, however, that opportunity to adapt was overlooked.

Dashed nationalist hopes of unity had at least 'been recompensed by prosperous conditions and by peace', as John E. Sayers, distinguished managing editor of the *Belfast Telegraph*, observed in 1955.[3] The peace to which he referred had in fact just been somewhat breached for, after a relative absence of physical-force activity, the IRA had reannounced itself with two daring arms raids in 1954. What had seemed isolated and futile incidents were seen later as the precursor of a sustained assault on the Northern state, announced as such in a manifesto in December 1956. It was an abortive exercise, in the event, with numerous incidents in the early months, followed by a desultory defensive exercise until the campaign was called off with recrimination in March 1962. The IRA itself blamed nationalists in the North for not supporting it, surely a sign that 'prosperity and peace' were preferred to the dubious charms of Dublin and the risks associated with direct action. The disdain of the nationalist electorate was given further outlet in the general election of 1959. Sinn Fein, the political wing of the physical-force movement, which chose to contest all twelve Westminster seats in that year as it had done in 1955, polled only 74,000 votes, less than half the 152,000 of the previous occasion.[4]

The fact that Costello's government cracked down hard on the IRA in the Republic and that when de Valera returned to power in 1957 he too pulled no punches also had significance. Indeed it was by his introduction of internment in July of that year and his matching of the Northern government's efforts to destroy what was seen on both sides of the border to be an unacceptable challenge to constitutional authority that the IRA was so swiftly rendered impotent.

Established governments have always an interest in preserving their own monopoly of force, and it was natural that there should be co-operation in the quelling of this challenge. Happily, in these years co-operation proved natural also in other areas.

As early as 1950, the Erne Drainage Development Act (NI) and the Republic's legislation of the same name illustrated the capacity of the two governments to pick up where they had left off before the war and to implement schemes of mutual benefit, in this instance a jointly funded scheme which involved major drainage works in Fermanagh and the development of hydro-electric power in Donegal. The following year, as the *Annual Register* observed, the two governments 'extended their co-operation in the economic sphere',[5] in spite of the continued bitterness of the constitutional issue. In 1952 they purchased jointly the Irish Society's salmon fisheries and agreed to administer them by a Foyle Fisheries Commission, established with equal representation from each jurisdiction and with responsibility for protection and conservation in this border area and for the management of fishing rights.

In 1953 it was the necessity of ensuring an efficient rail service between Dublin and Belfast that brought both parties together, this time to create the Great Northern Railway Board. Since the beginning of both states this link had required official co-operation and there had been negotiations in progress for some years to try to put the service on a viable footing. The new Board proved but a temporary step, lasting only until 1958, when separate, publicly-owned companies took over responsibility for a shared service that has since stood the test of time.

In day-to-day matters, especially those requiring working solutions to border problems, the two governments could thus prove to be good neighbours, whatever acrimony was being expressed at the highest levels. From customs control and cross-border trade and traffic, to lighthouse administration, the control of foot and mouth disease, the supply of electricity or the registration of veterinary surgeons, arrangements were worked out with greater or less publicity. And as the ravages of war receded, so the range of such matters increased. As year succeeded year during the early fifties, the same phrases occurred in the *Annual Register's* summary of events: intergovernmental contacts were distinguished by 'amicable co-operation', 'friendly co-operation', 'friendly relations'. Even when the IRA campaign intruded its headlines there was appreciation noted for the energetic steps taken by the Dublin government to deal severely with this menace.

The Irish Catholic Church, it is true, remained conservative: an attempt was made to cancel a football match between the Republic and Yugoslavia, a communist country noted for its Church persecution, in Dublin in 1955; in 1957 an anti-Protestant boycott in the Wexford village of Fethard-on-Sea, over a mixed-marriage breach of educational undertakings, received strong Church support, and both, to be sure, provided self-righteous condemnation from northern spokesmen. Yet the football match went ahead and though it lacked State recognition it was viewed by a large crowd; and the Fethard boycott was roundly condemned by the then Taoiseach, Mr de Valera. Even the management of the Church was subject to change. In 1958, at the centre, a liberalising Pope John 23 (1958–62) began moves, carried further in the Second Vatican Council (1962–5), that were to open up the Church to more public debate, to more open practices, and to greater lay participation.

The year 1958 was also important internally, in the Republic, for it witnessed the publication of *Economic Development*, a far-reaching analysis of an economy which had seen no rise in GNP since 1953 and which required major overhaul if it was to compete in the expanding world of new economies and disappearing trade barriers. Economic planning was set in train with the country's First Programme for Economic Expansion, covering the period ahead from 1959 to 1963.

In June 1959 this was matched by political change. Eamon de Valera finally quit active politics to become President, and Sean Lemass replaced him as Taoiseach. The Irish Republic was set to enter the 1960s in better fettle. Its determination to attract investment, and its conversion to outward-looking policies and a free-trade philosophy would inevitably have repercussions for Northern Ireland in the decade ahead.

It was in the 1960s that the Republic finally threw off the shackles of protectionism and wartime stagnation, transformed its economy and prepared itself to take its place in the newly emerging European Community. Tractors on the farm, cars on the road, and telephones and televisions in the home all increased dramatically from the close of the 1950s – the latter, in particular, enlarging awareness of the outside world. The final acceptance of Ireland into membership of the United Nations in 1955, the joining of the IMF and the World Bank in 1957, and GATT in 1960, all contributed to this process, but it was television, received at first tentatively from Britain, more readily from BBC NI from 1953, but most directly and widely once Irish Television (RTE) began broadcasting in 1962, that brought the outside world, with its challenging range of standards, values and norms, to the attention of the Irish people. The Republic's initial bid for entry into the Common Market in 1961 lapsed with the veto of the United Kingdom's application in 1963, but when the two countries succeeded in joining on 1 January 1973, for Ireland, the interval of expansion had proved beneficial; or, at the very least, 'the ten year delay eased the pains of transition'.[6]

The sixties decade then, was to change both parts of Ireland considerably, and it was to affect not least their mutual relations. It was Lemass who assisted the processes in the Republic, freeing up trade, with concessions to certain Northern Irish goods with his first liberalisation of trade in 1962, and concluding a more far-reaching Anglo-Irish Free Trade Agreement in 1965 that had further benefits north of the border; introducing the successful, seven-year Second Programme for Economic Development in 1963, which would continue the 4 per cent growth of the First, increase the standard of living by 50 per cent and reverse the emigration outflow; and, even more spectacularly, breaking the mould early in 1965 by journeying to Belfast to meet his counterpart, Terence O'Neill.

O'Neill had replaced the ageing Brooke (Lord Brookeborough since 1952) in 1963 and had set himself a similar task of modernisation; but here attention was focused on political structures and sectional relationships which had lagged so far behind material advance. Nervous of the reaction of his political colleagues, he was willing nevertheless to meet Lemass and to discuss practical matters of mutual concern, and even to return the historic 14 January meeting with a visit to Dublin on 9 February. His objective, in his own later words, 'was to promote a decent, sane, neighbourly relationship'.[7]

Lemass the pragmatist had long argued that the best way to win eventual unity was by attraction, by improving the material well-being of the Republic's citizens and by removing aspects of its political and social life that were distasteful to Protestant opinion. The Second Programme (superseded by a Third in 1967), did much for the former, and because the latter included elements of the 1937 Constitution, Lemass initiated and chaired, shortly before his retirement in 1967, an all-Party Committee on this fundamental document. This recommended the deletion or alteration of key articles referring to the special position of the Roman Catholic Church, the non-availability of divorce and the territorial claim to Northern Ireland. In the event, under Lemass's successor, Jack Lynch (1967–79), only the first was effected but Lemass himself witnessed the liberalisation of censorship of both films (1964) and books (1967).

It was unfortunate for the better understanding that Prime Ministerial meetings began to generate that the triumphalist celebration of the fiftieth anniversary of the 1916 Rising followed so swiftly on their heels and offended Northern Unionist sensibilities once more. Lemass was an honourable exception to the euphoric, irredentist mood but some of the events set in train were to reverberate disastrously before the decade was out. O'Neill and Lynch, who got off to a good personal start with a similar exchange of meetings, in Belfast in December 1967 and in Dublin in January 1968, were left to deal with a deteriorating situation in the province, which finally erupted into violence towards the end of the latter year.

O'Neill had seemed to begin well as Premier of Northern Ireland. Brookeborough had lingered too long and on all sides there seemed to be an expectation of political initiatives to match those in the economic and social spheres. In fact it was the continuing needs of the economy that first received attention, but problems of trade union recognition and of employment practices quickly led to a greater focus on matters political.

An Economic Council, set up in August 1963, could not function until the political inhibitions over recognising the Dublin-based Irish Congress of Trade Unions had been overcome; the attraction of foreign firms required an end to some of the more sophisticated local habits of job discrimination. In 1964 the deadlock in the first of these was resolved with the government's recognition of the ICTU's Northern Ireland Committee and the advisory Economic

Council thus came into being. Its first task was to look at Belfast's own latest move towards planning, *Economic Development in Northern Ireland*, submitted by Professor Tom Wilson of Glasgow University in December 1964, though not revealed to the public until February 1965.

When a *Times* Special Supplement on Northern Ireland was issued in April 1965, it was possible to look back on the meeting of Prime Ministers, which had broken 'a 40-year deadlock', with some optimism. Catholics in the province welcomed the summit, it observed, but also many 'enlightened Unionists' who saw, with their Prime Minister, 'that over and above the necessity of trade and tourism, the issues of religion and the border must become less vibrant'. Yet, when the paper's correspondent toured the countryside he had to observe that 'the signs of improvement in general atmosphere and tolerance are few, and mainly noticeable in the eastern counties. . . . Travelling in the western and southern counties it is impossible not to feel the heat of nationalist feelings.'[8]

Not least amongst western grievances was the suspicion that economic development was being deliberately confined to the more Unionist east, and while the government had some defence on this issue, in that incoming firms were inclined for transport and market reasons to insist on an eastern location, it had a less convincing answer to the outrage of local nationalists and unionists alike when it decided to locate Ulster's second university in Unionist Coleraine rather than in the largely nationalist Londonderry, the province's second city and seat already of a suitable basis, Magee University College.

What was obvious to the *Times* writer was that 'to the problems of development there is no more of a quick answer than there is to the religious–political question. They both need time.' Lemass and O'Neill had started a process and in the spring of 1965 it was still possible to hope that the consequences flowing from this process 'can only be for the good'.[9] But things had been allowed to fester too long already and nationalist patience was coming to an end. Time was a boon that was not to be granted to O'Neill.

details of the descent into violence in Northern Ireland
read about elsewhere and are relevant here only in so far
y affected Belfast–Dublin relations. In 1966 the cordiality
or these relations, coupled with the 1916 anniversary celebrations, increased the anxiety and the stridency of the more
extreme Unionists, which in turn made it harder for the
government to respond to the increasingly articulate demands
of the nationalist community for full equality of citizenship
within the new, modern, welfare-state province. To that community, the form in which Northern Ireland had been created
had left it in a position of permanent, impotent minority. Post-
war change had brought greater health, education and social-
welfare benefits, but opportunities for the nationalist people to
participate in the shaping of the society in which they lived, or
even to nourish Irish language and culture, had not improved.
Now in the late 1960s, an era of international concern for civil
rights and for the challenging of conservative societies,
northern nationalists took matters into their own hands.

In January 1967 a Northern Ireland Civil Rights Association
was formed and demands for an end to discriminatory
practices and for action to promote nationalist interests
moved onto the streets in marches and meetings. By the
following year, marches were generating counter-marches as
Protestant and Unionist extremists, spearheaded by the
intransigent Ian Paisley, denounced the largely Catholic civil
rights enthusiasts as republican irredentists in another guise.
Civil rights demands had substance, however, and they were
listed late in 1968 without any need to resort to the language
of nationalism: 'one man one vote' in local council elections;
the ending of gerrymandered boundaries; laws to prevent
discrimination by local authorities, and a complaints pro-
cedure; allocation of public housing according to a points
system; repeal of the Special Powers Act; and disbandment of
the 'B' Special reserve constabulary, seen as a purely
Protestant, intimidatory force.[10]

Lynch and O'Neill could talk greater co-operation, for
example in tourism, trade and electricity supply (the two

governments had in 1965 established a joint committee in regard to the latter and in 1967 had concluded an agreement on connecting the two state electricity undertakings), but it was Northern Ireland's internal matters that would dictate the pace and dominate attention from this point onwards.

Once again it was in Londonderry that matters came to a head. On 5 October 1968 a NICRA-sponsored but locally organised march in the city was banned by Home Affairs Minister William Craig. The march went ahead despite the ban and encountered harsh police reaction. The brutal batoning of marchers, including well-known political figures, was captured by television cameras and beamed immediately around the world. The Northern Ireland troubles had reached take-off. Taoiseach Lynch felt impelled to put the blame for the province's ills on Partition itself, to the annoyance of O'Neill, who accused his opposite number in Dublin of intervening in Northern Ireland's domestic affairs.[11]

Further marches created tension in the province until, on 11 December, a month's moratorium was called by the Derry Citizen's Action Committee. 1968 was a year of student protest internationally, however, and Peoples' Democracy, a largely student organisation begun at Queen's University early in October, decided to set aright its own part of the world by defying this attempt to cool passions down. Its more active members marched from Belfast to Derry from 1 to 4 January 1969, stimulating opposition of the most violent and bigotted kind. At Burntollet Bridge on 4 January, organised attacks on the marchers came to a head, with no apparent objection (to put it mildly) from the forces of law and order. The injured, bedraggled survivors reached Derry later that day in the glare of outraged publicity. The chance of a reflective breathing space and a de-fusing of tension had vanished. Community relations within the province plummeted, splits within Unionism widened and O'Neill failed to strengthen his position at a general election held for that purpose on 24 February 1969. By 28 April he had given up the lost cause, being replaced as Prime Minister by James Chichester-Clark on 1 May.

In August 1969 sectarian fighting became so intense in Londonderry and Belfast and the police so exhausted that ten thousand troops were despatched from Britain to aid the civil power. Again the Republic's Prime Minister spoke out. Though unable to take positive action, other than moving army units and field hospitals to the border area, he promised that his government would 'not stand by', and reasserted his condemnation of present and previous Northern Irish governments.[12] Inevitably, intergovernmental relations deteriorated. Furthermore, the government at Westminster, for almost fifty years content to ignore the management of Northern Ireland, found itself dragged into active involvement in the province's affairs.

That involvement was to become total in 1972, when the steady deterioration in security and the inability of the government in Belfast any longer to maintain law and order provoked London into suspending the Belfast administration (initially for one year but in practice indefinitely), and assuming direct responsibility itself. In vain the governments of Chichester-Clark (May 1969–March 1971) and Faulkner (March 1971–March 1972) legislated to remove grievances, to provide the structures of equality, and the machinery to receive complaints and enforce judgements: measures that could be put in place with relative speed but which needed time to demonstrate results and even more time to change permanently a dominant political culture established over successive generations.

By 1972, inter-communal violence had helped to revivify the IRA, which in January 1970 had split to produce a militant Provisional (Provo) wing, willing to protect beleaguered Catholic nationalist areas but also committed to a programme of destruction, of life and property, designed to throw off 'British rule' for ever from this last territorial foothold in Ireland. The IRA, fronted politically by Sinn Fein, was a self-appointed destroyer with no mandate but with aims that coincided with those of the constitutionally elected representatives of nationalism in the North and throughout the island. Their means were unacceptable to such nationalists, however, and their deeds, destructive of goodwill as well as of life and property, were once again seen to be a threat to constitutional government in Dublin as well as in Belfast. Contributing, no doubt, to the ending of devolved government in Belfast, the IRA also generated determination amongst Protestant Unionists and London politicians alike not to see Northern Ireland bombed out of the United Kingdom. Early terrorist success turned counter-productive in the longer term. And the defeat of terrorism became an interest shared equally on both sides of the border.

This had become apparent before 1972. As early as 1970 Dublin had been the scene of an alleged arms conspiracy involving Cabinet Ministers Charles Haughey and Neil Blaney. Both men were dismissed in May, and the former endured a trial, at which he was acquitted, in October. The alleged conspiracy related to the sending of arms to Catholic groups in the North. The problem for the Dublin government was that determining what to do to help these people, or to calm the situation, was difficult. Posturing achieved little, and after President Hillery had made an unannounced visit to Belfast and appealed unrealistically for United Nations intervention in 1970 (both the cause of diplomatic pique), Prime Minister Lynch resumed his recognition of the fact that the Protestant community in the North had some rights and that Irish unity would require an accommodation of those rights in new constitutional arrangements. In the meantime, he argued (Feb 1972), there was a need within Northern Ireland for some form of power-sharing between Unionists and the Nationalist representatives.[13]

There had been developments during this period, too, affecting those representatives. The immense pressure of events had produced a more effective coming together of constitutional nationalists as well as causing splits and regroupings amongst their Unionist opponents.

On 21 August 1970, most of the supporters of the old Nationalist Party, the National Democratic Party and the Republican Labour Party had merged into the Social Democratic and Labour Party (SDLP), under the leadership of Gerry Fitt, MP, and with half a dozen other prominent Stormont politicians, including John Hume, Austin Currie and Paddy Devlin. The SDLP was to prove enduring and well organised, putting forward a left-of-centre programme seeking full civil rights, better North–South relations and eventual Irish unity, though it expressed itself ready in the meantime to work for the better participation of its adherents in the decision-making processes of Northern Ireland.

On the pro-union side, the messy nature of O'Neill's failure had helped in the creation of an Alliance Party, in April 1970: from the outset a party determined to draw upon Catholic and Protestant support for the existing constitutional relationship with Britain. O'Neillite Unionists and former supporters of the Northern Ireland Labour Party were amongst its early members, and it gained three sitting Stormont MPs in 1972 when two Unionists (Phelim O'Neill and Bertie McConnell) and one Nationalist (Joe Gormley) joined its ranks. Under the leadership of Oliver Napier, it appealed to all religious persuasions to stand together within the union, and sought a reconstituted legislative assembly and the involvement of both communities at all levels of government within the province.

More ominous for the traditionalist Unionist representation was the formation in September 1971 of the Democratic Unionist Party (DUP). Founded by Desmond Boal, the Stormont MP for Shankill, and the Revd Ian Paisley, it embraced the latter's Protestant Unionist Party, already boasting two MPs at Stormont, including Paisley himself who had captured Terence O'Niell's old constituency, Bannside, in April 1970. The DUP was quickly dominated by Paisley, who derided the faint-hearted and compromising Unionist establishment and consistently advocated strong, populist demands for a return to 'democratic' local government which would recognise the predominance of Unionist numbers.

Early in 1972, these divisions within Unionism had persuaded William Craig, the former Home Affairs Minister, to establish Ulster Vanguard as a loyalist umbrella group, but if anything this served simply to add to the number of alternative centres of Unionist action. At the same time Brian

Faulkner was presiding over the last stages of Unionist rule. The marked deterioration of 1971, with robberies and killings and bombings a feature of everyday life, had given way in 1972 to what was to become 'the worst year in Northern Ireland's history'.[14] The sequence of dramatically bloody incidents, which contributed to record levels of dead and injured, began in earnest with the shooting dead of 13 marchers by soldiers of the parachute regiment in Derry on 30 January ('Bloody Sunday'). In immediate reaction, an angry mob burned down the British embassy in Dublin on 2 February. In the slightly longer term, the Westminster government decided to assume full responsibility for security in Northern Ireland, leading to the resignation of the Faulkner government and, on 30 March, to the suspension for a year (in fact it was to prove permanent) of the Stormont parliament.

Fifty years of devolved government had not provided a lasting solution to the Irish problem, nor created a climate conducive to the merging of responsibilities within an Irish or a British sovereignty. Within Northern Ireland there had been created instead an image of the old all-island situation, writ small: a militant minority within a predominantly alien majority which appeared unassailably entrenched and unlikely to respond to minority wishes. Recent years had witnessed a minority resort to direct action, in despair of constitutional institutions. This too had been rebuffed, though in practice many steps had been taken to remove initial civil rights grievances. Nevertheless, civil rights activists had been condemned as nationalists-by-another-name, a condemnation which in turn forced many back to nationalism as the only path left by which to pursue full justice, so apparently justifying their detractors. But now Westminster had seized back power. Could it find a better solution, by way of reconciliation or by imposition?

7

LONDON STEPS IN:
1972–92

The assumption of direct responsibility for Northern Irish affairs by Westminster in March 1972 inevitably altered the relationship between the two parts of Ireland. A new and major player had entered the field. Northern Irish views could still be expressed publicly, but the official conduct of relations with Dublin had passed to the British government, most notably to the new Secretary of State for Northern Ireland, and his accompanying Ministers, all appointed by that government. A much greater emphasis on Ministerial (and in particular Prime Ministerial) meetings, more in London and Dublin than in Belfast, took matters beyond the reach of the elected representatives of the province. These latter frequently felt marginalised, while their constituents found it impossible to call their governors to account. The national parties were not represented in Northern Ireland, so governments, Labour or Conservative, could act without regard to electoral opinion on the ground.

That, it could be argued, was just what was needed. Devolved government had failed. It was time for wiser and more lofty minds to address the issues: to identify·basic requirements and to devise structures to embody them.

Under William Whitelaw, the first Northern Ireland Secretary, some essentials for a harmonious future were quickly established. The old Westminster-style majority-rule Stormont would not do. There must be a proper sharing of power between majority and minority representatives if power was again to be devolved to Belfast. In an artificially contrived polity, with a built-in, permanent, Unionist majority, talk of democracy by 'majority rule' was misleading. Furthermore, it soon came to be accepted by the new masters that recognition of a role for the nationalist community implied recognition of the broader 'Irish dimension', no matter how unpalatable this might be to Unionists.

By 1980 Northern Ireland's 'Irish dimension' had begun to be pushed further. Dublin, so long frustrated at its exclusion from decision-making in the North, had been seeking an input that would at least protect the interests of the minority, nationalist community there. Now it started to call for a broader Irish solution to be considered, leading during the 1980s to demands for an examination of the 'totality of relationships' between Britain and Ireland, and for studies to be undertaken and structures devised to promote co-operation, defeat terrorism, and reach a permanent settlement in the North itself.

To a continuing backdrop of paramilitary violence in the province, spilling over from time to time into the Republic and into Britain, studies were completed, structures were devised and efforts were made to bring to agreement the constitutional representatives of the Ulster people. The unionist camp, divided into quarrelling parties (Ulster Unionist, Democratic Unionist, and Alliance), and divided at times even within individual parties, faced, in the Social Democratic and Labour Party, the most effective nationalist party since the foundation of the state, though it too was confronted by extremist opposition, notably Sinn Fein, within the nationalist community.

In Dublin there was considerable difference of emphasis between the two main parties. Fine Gael, under the leadership of Garret FitzGerald from July 1977, recognised that the Republic must put its own house in order, to accommodate a Unionist community little attracted by the present southern state. Fianna Fail, led by Charles Haughey from December 1979, was more inclined to seek unilateral action from London, in its view the source and paymaster of partition, than to deal directly with Unionists, though it issued repeated assurances that it was ready to listen to Unionist proposals.

An unbroken period of Conservative rule in London, with Margaret Thatcher Prime Minister from May 1979, meant a measure of continuity, and there was also an underlying consensus between the two main British parties on the priority of defeating terrorism and effecting power-sharing devolution in Northern Ireland. The Labour Party, however, committed itself to the longer-term objective of Irish unity by consent, and was not happy with some anti-terrorist measures.

In these circumstances, an account of Belfast–Dublin relations must shift gear and context. In what is a closing chronological chapter on an open-ended topic, emphasis will be placed on the major landmarks of a continuing journey of exploration, with some focus on the major players, and with some regard to those events which revealed the priorities and the perceptions of peoples north and south. All the while, though, contacts and co-operation, despite occasional reverses, continued across the Irish border, and across the Irish Sea: extensive co-operation in economic affairs (transport, gas, electricity, trade, tourism, regional development, employment); and in security matters (police and army, extradition, courts and judiciary, anti-terrorism strategies); and not a little debate, and some action, in the political realm, especially regarding the rights of the citizen (reciprocal voting; attitudes towards homosexuality, contraception, divorce, and abortion).

Chronologically, the period opened with the determination of the first Northern Ireland Secretary, William Whitelaw, to achieve an executive body made up of representatives of both traditional unionism and nationalism. The fact that the SDLP had committed itself to Irish unity by consent, and that consent was not immediately available, meant that it was prepared in the short term to work to develop Northern Ireland itself into a more harmonious society, though in September 1972 it did call for the British and Irish governments to agree on a form of joint sovereignty to provide the appropriate context for such development. The following month the British government went so far as to recognise the Irish dimension of the problem. Terrorism escalated, however, and the year ended with a record 467 violent deaths to underline the necessity of political co-operation.

The adhesion of both the United Kingdom and the Republic to the European Economic Community on 1 January 1973 seemed to bode well for the spirit of joint endeavour, and during that year plans were evolved to translate aspiration into action. First, a Border Poll was conducted in Northern Ireland on 8 March to clarify views regarding sovereignty, and the majority wish to remain British was confirmed, those in favour, in a 58.5 per cent turn-out, totalling 591,820; those against 6,463. An SDLP call to boycott the proceedings clearly reduced the latter figure, but even allowing generous interpretation, it must be inferred that 20–25 per cent of the minority community voted for continued inclusion in the United Kingdom.[1] Then, on 20 March, a White Paper, *Constitutional Proposals for Northern Ireland*, recommended a return to devolution, with power-sharing in an Assembly with specific local responsibilities, and a Council of Ireland to institutionalise regular consultation between Belfast and Dublin. Voting took place on 28 June to elect the Assembly, whose 78 members convened on 31 July.

After a September meeting between Premiers Heath and Cosgrave to pledge support for a Council of Ireland, agreement was reached in principle on 5 October between Unionist, SDLP and Alliance leaders to share power. Form was put on this controversial agreement on 21 November, when the party allocation of 11 posts was announced (6 Unionist, 4 SDLP, 1 Alliance), with Brian Faulkner as Chief Executive, and Gerry Fitt his Deputy. Strenuous opposition had been voiced from the beginning by hard-line Unionists, however, who denounced the deal as a 'betrayal', while the IRA described the SDLP as 'arch collaborators' and promised an intensification of 'the armed struggle'.

When representatives of the Executive and the British and Irish governments met at Sunningdale, from 6 to 9 December, and agreed formally to establish a Council of Ireland, however, Unionist hard-line hostility knew no bounds, despite a commitment of both sovereign governments to respect the wishes of the majority in Northern Ireland in regard to any change of constitutional status in the province. The Executive could not expect an easy ride when it took up its responsibilities on 1 January 1974.

By the time it faced the Assembly, on 21 January, a majority of the Ulster Unionist Council had rejected Faulkner's stance, forcing him to lead his Assembly supporters into a separate, pro-Executive 'Unionist Party of Northern Ireland' (UPNI). Meanwhile, three days before the Sunningdale Conference, the popular Whitelaw, needed back at base, had been replaced by Francis Pym as Secretary of State, a move deprecated by all the other participants. This clear evidence of London priorities was further emphasised when Edward Heath called a general election for 28 February. It may have seemed necessary to him to establish his authority at Westminster, but the political upheaval, in which he in fact lost out to Labour, came too early in the life of the Executive. The clear voter statement in Northern Ireland of lack of confidence in Faulkner's party weakened it fatally. Unionists in general rejected the Council of Ireland as a threat to the Union. They were also alarmed at the pace and intensity of Belfast–Dublin and Dublin–London exchanges in these weeks and returned anti-Sunningdale candidates in eleven of the twelve Westminster seats, the twelfth going to Fitt.

In May, a widespread strike called by the Ulster Workers Council, which lasted from 15 to 29 of the month, forced the resignation of the Executive on 28 May and the abandonment, for the time being at least, of the hopeful experiment of power-sharing. The experience had been valuable to all participants, not least the SDLP, representing a community hitherto excluded from any participation in decision-making, but its life had been too brief for conclusions to be drawn with any degree of certainty.

Under Prime Minister Harold Wilson, the commitment to the principles of power-sharing and a special relationship with Dublin were re-affirmed: with the SDLP on 10 September 1974, and Taoiseach Liam Cosgrave the following day. The Labour Northern Ireland Secretary, Merlyn Rees, had by then announced a further assembly for the province, this time a Convention to draw up alternative plans to implement these principles. Dominated as it was, however, by Unionists who sought a return to majority-rule devolution, it failed to satisfy this purpose when it delivered its Report in November 1975. It was eventually wound up in March 1976. In the following month Wilson resigned, being replaced by James Callaghan.

A change of leadership occurred in the Republic also, in June 1977, when Lynch and Fianna Fail returned to power. His main contribution in Opposition had been to call for 'an ordered withdrawal' by Britain from Northern Ireland (29 October 1975), a sentiment echoed by the Catholic Primate, Archbishop O'Fiach (later, on 30 June 1979, elevated to Cardinal) early in 1978. Cosgrave was replaced as Fine Gael leader by Garret FitzGerald on 1 July 1977, and, in contrast, his contribution in 1978 was to observe that Protestants in Northern Ireland would be fools to join the Republic under its present constitution (11 February).[2]

Anglo-Irish relations were once more transformed by the success, this time to prove protracted, of Margaret Thatcher's Conservatives in May 1979. The tough Roy Mason, who had replaced Rees as Northern Ireland Secretary in September 1977, was now, in 1979, in turn replaced by Humphrey Atkins. Other players, too, changed during this significant year. The Ulster Unionists, having survived a number of challenges, consolidated under the leadership of James Molyneaux in September. For a long period under his leadership, however, they were to be divided between enthusiasts for devolution on the one hand, and on the other those favouring total integration into the United Kingdom (heavily influenced by Enoch Powell, who had become Unionist MP for South Down in 1974). The second focus for Unionism, the DUP, remained a significant force and when the first direct elections to the European Parliament occurred in June 1979, its leader Ian Paisley topped the poll. John Hume took another of the three seats and in November he formally became leader of the SDLP, a party he had for some time dominated.

Gerry Fitt resigned the SDLP leadership, in fact, protesting that too much stress was being placed on Dublin at the expense of matters within the province. An increased role for Dublin, for example, had been the burden of an SDLP proposal (*Towards a New Ireland*) earlier in the month, seeking a joint British–Irish approach to the Northern Ireland problem. On 5 December that thrust was strengthened by the resignation of Lynch and the appointment, two days later, of Charles Haughey as Fianna Fail Taoiseach.

Increasingly in 1980, the running was made at top level, with Haughey in February calling for a British–Irish initiative and in May meeting with Thatcher in London to discuss the 'unique relationship' between their two countries. In Dublin, in December, it was felt that the 'totality of the relationship between these islands' should be reviewed, and studies were commissioned 'covering possible new institutional relationships, citizenship rights, security matters, economic co-operation and measures to encourage mutual understanding'.[3]

During 1981, a year dominated by IRA hunger strikes in Belfast and the death of ten of these republican prisoners through starvation, reports on the above studies were completed, being laid before both parliaments on 11 November. By this time Garret FitzGerald had succeeded Haughey as Taoiseach (30 June 1981). On 6 November he had held talks with Mrs Thatcher about their implementation, including the establishment of an Anglo-Irish Ministerial Council, a Secretariat formed of designated civil servants, an inter-parliamentary body, and an Advisory Committee on economic, social and cultural co-operation. They agreed to make a start by creating the first of these bodies, and when they met again, on 7 November 1983 (after a second, brief, Haughey administration from April to November 1982), they deemed this latter encounter to be the first meeting of the Intergovernmental Council at Heads of Government level. Ministers, in the meantime, had been consulting since January 1982, and a non-governmental body, Anglo-Irish Encounter, with joint Chairmen in London and Dublin (Sir David Orr and Dr T. K. Whitaker, respectively), had been established in July 1983 to promote economic, social and cultural exchange. Anglo-Irish, and by extension Northern Irish–Irish, relations were being forwarded by decisions well beyond the reach of Northern Ireland's Unionist representatives, a fact made even less palatable to them by the apparent success of the SDLP leader John Hume in setting the agenda. In December 1982, for example, he had publicly called for nationalist political parties throughout Ireland to draw up a blueprint for the state they desired, a call which seemed to meet with a swift response.

Garret FitzGerald, sensitive to Unionist reaction and long convinced of the inappropriateness of the present Irish Constitution for an eventual state incorporating all the island's peoples, had himself embarked on a fundamental reassessment of nationalist goals. Calling together representatives of constitutional nationalism, North as well as South, and inviting Unionists also to participate, he sought early in 1983 to create the means to marginalise the men of violence, to comprehend and remove the fears of Unionists, and to map out the contours of a future United Ireland, to be achieved 'peacefully and by consent'.[4]

On 30 May 1983 he launched his New Ireland Forum in Dublin. The process of hearing and weighing evidence from a wide range of political and other opinions, including some unofficial Unionist witnesses anxious that their perspective be not ignored, lasted a full year, the Report appearing on 2 May 1984. It was a succinct summary of options, favouring an all-island unitary state, but recognising other possibilities such as a federal or confederal state, joint sovereignty over Northern Ireland, or indeed any other solution that might yet be identified that would accommodate both traditions in Northern Ireland and which could be 'freely negotiated and agreed to by the people of the North and by the people of the South'.[5]

While Irishmen had been discussing their preferred future, Englishmen had been absolved from action, but once the Forum Report had been published it behoved London to respond. A two-day summit at Chequers, on 18 and 19 November 1984, encouraged Unionists when Prime Minister Thatcher decisively dismissed all the proposed options. But this first reaction in the event proved misleading. A further Prime Ministerial meeting in December hinted that officials were busy preparing a comprehensive agreement between the two countries. Unionists grew uneasy.

Unionists had been chivvied into action earlier by Secretary of State James Prior, who had succeeded Atkins in September 1981, and who had set in motion what was termed 'rolling devolution' in a White Paper in April 1982. This envisaged a consultative Assembly of 78 members to monitor legislation, in the first instance, and later to assume a measure of power, once cross-community confidence had been established. With its sights on a wider Irish solution, however, the SDLP had refused to take its seats, and with Sinn Fein also boycotting, the Assembly was left to the Unionist and Alliance Parties. They had worked conscientiously to make devolution possible, recognising the validity of minority rights, proposing a Human Rights Commission to give weight to such rights and, in October 1985, approving a return to power-sharing.

Others, too, had been giving thought to Northern Ireland's problems. In November 1984, a committee representative of mainline British and Northern Irish political thinking and chaired by Lord Kilbrandon had issued a report in favour of 'co-operative devolution' and seeking formal recognition from Dublin of the legitimacy of Northern Ireland.[6] Then, in 1985, an inter-party Commission of the short-lived Liberal/Social Democratic Party Alliance, chaired by Lord Donaldson, had recommended executive devolution, backed by a British–Irish Parliamentary Council (along Nordic Council lines) and a British–Irish Security Commission.[7] But it was the secret, high-level, joint committee of British and Irish civil servants who had the actual responsibility and it was their bombshell that burst upon the Unionist community at Hillsborough on 15 November 1985.

Growing apprehension had led leaders of the two main Unionist Parties, both in a press statement in Belfast at the beginning of October and after a meeting with Mrs Thatcher in London at the end of the month, to warn the government on no account to grant Dublin even a consultative role in the affairs of the province. Yet that is precisely what Margaret Thatcher and Garret FitzGerald agreed to do in the Anglo-Irish Agreement signed on 15 November: a role to be delivered through an intergovernmental conference backed by a secretariat in Belfast staffed by civil servants from both countries. A divided Unionism, deemed incapable of dealing adequately with an alienated minority, had paid the price of its division. The two sovereign governments acted to thwart the ambitions of the violent opponents of the SDLP, to break the deadlock in the Northern Ireland Assembly, and to bring constitutional nationalists into the decision-making process while at the same time legitimising their cultural and political aspirations.

Outrage, panic and hysteria marked the Unionist response to an Agreement[8] which actually guaranteed to respect majority opinion regarding any change in Northern Ireland's constitutional status and provided a mechanism by which to achieve devolution but which was perceived as a betrayal of the Union. Consisting of a Preamble and 13 Articles, the Agreement (see Appendix F for the full text) expressed the determination of the two governments to bring peace and stability to the province by reconciling the two communities there through dialogue, mutual respect, the ending of discrimination and the promotion of common participation in the processes of government. By permitting the Irish government to oversee the interests of the minority pending devolution, however, and to advise on the composition of various nominated bodies, on internal security and prison policy, law enforcement and extradition, and on cross-border co-operation in security, economic, social and cultural matters, it blinded Unionists to its positive aspects.

Tom King, Secretary of State from 1 September 1985 (replacing Douglas Hurd, who had in turn succeeded Prior in September 1984), had the task of selling the Agreement to the majority in the province and he attempted in vain to do so by urging a careful reading and a recognition of the support and opportunity which it gave. Their politicians, however, closed ranks and converted the Assembly into a Grand Committee with the sole purpose of finding ways to subvert the Agreement. The Unionist MPs then took the initiative and, resigning en bloc on 15 December, went to their constituents on 23 January 1986 in what they argued was a referendum on the Agreement.

They sought to total half a million voters in their support. In the event they gathered 418,239, and suffered the humiliation of losing one of their seats, in Newry–Armagh, to SDLP Deputy Leader, Seamus Mallon. Even so, their performance on a wet winter's day was not unimpressive and it ushered in a new phase of ill-tempered and intemperate division within the province. On 23 June the Assembly was dissolved, it being clearly out of step with its original purpose, but the devolution intended by the Agreement did not follow. Vehement Unionist reaction had produced the worst of all worlds: Direct Rule into which the Dublin government could inject advice at regular intervals. It was a situation that was to prove agreeable to their main rivals, the SDLP, and it was a situation destined to persist.

The year 1986 was one of resentment in Northern Unionist circles, with the Anglo-Irish Agreement being implemented on the ground and with the first intergovernmental Conference in Dublin taking place in mid-October. Meanwhile a constitutional referendum in the Republic on 26 June rejected divorce, a move in keeping with a twenty-six rather than a thirty-two county mentality.[9] But not everything was negative. A Unionist call at the end of January for a tripartite Conference on all the relationships between Britain, the Republic and Northern Ireland, had implied some readiness to try to talk through existing differences. And in the following year further thought emerged from the paramilitary wing of Unionism as well as from a specialist group established by the two main Unionist political parties.

Of these latter initiatives, it was the Political Research Group of the Ulster Defence Association that had acted first, producing a document, *Common Sense*,[10] which faced up to the new realities, turned away from previous flirtations with an 'independent' Northern Ireland and recommended a permanent, devolved, power-sharing coalition as its preferred government for the province; a recommendation perhaps more interesting in terms of where it was coming from than what it contained. The July 1987 report[11] of the Task Force set up by Official and Democratic Unionists the previous February was a different matter, with some hard-hitting substance and a recognition that Unionist resistance to the Hillsborough accord was degenerating into an unacceptable shambles.

Entitled *An End to Drift*, and authored by OUP General Secretary Frank Millar, DUP Deputy Leader Peter Robinson, and the OUP MP for Upper Bann, Harold McCusker, the report welcomed the earlier *Common Sense* and developed its own argument for 'politics' rather than 'protest'. Following the lead given by the UDA, and also major Presbyterian and Church of Ireland figures earlier in the year, who had argued that mere negative obstruction would not suffice; and responding as well to some encouragement from senior SDLP figures that there was room for discussion, the Task Force sought a devolutionary solution that would eliminate Dublin's direct intervention in Northern Irish affairs. Party leaders Molyneaux and Paisley seemed unenthusiastic, however, and the moment for action was allowed to pass.

The horrific IRA bomb at the war memorial in Enniskillen, exploding before the Remembrance Service on 8 November 1987, and killing eleven civilians, did little to encourage inter-communal warmth or to improve relations between Belfast and Dublin. The year ended, however, with further attention to one of the truly central concerns of both capitals, and of London too: extradition. This had long been one of those security issues clouded by different perceptions in each jurisdiction. On 23 November, in a move not unconnected with the wave of public outrage at the Enniskillen massacre, the Dublin government altered its law to conform to the 1977 European Convention on the Suppression of Terrorism, to which it had agreed to subscribe when it signed the

Anglo-Irish Agreement two years earlier at Hillsborough. Commentators, however, did not foresee any major changes in practice following from the move.

Prime Ministerial talks on Northern Ireland continued during 1988 and 1989, to a background of calls for comprehensive discussions. In October 1988, the Alliance Party contributed its own analysis, *Governing with Consent*, which called for 'devolved, cross-community government, within the UK but recognising the Anglo-Irish context'.[12] The following July (1989), the patient Tom King was replaced as Northern Ireland Secretary by the avuncular Peter Brooke. He did his shrewd best as time went on to map out the common ground amongst the province's politicians, stressing the potential of devolution in January 1990, for example, then encouraging dialogue and reporting progress regularly to Dublin.

In the April of 1990, the Taoiseach, Charles Haughey, visited Belfast at the invitation of the Institute of Directors. He had earlier emphasised to Northerners his willingness to be generous in any all-Ireland settlement. On this occasion, eschewing party politics, he spoke of the 'wide range of initiatives which could be undertaken, cross-border, which would bring economic and social benefits to both parts of Ireland'. He urged the members of the audience and their Southern counterparts to adopt a wide range of joint measures, not least that they should 'explore common branding of products, shared market information and research and joint overseas marketing initiatives'. Such developments, he argued, 'will create a new Irish economic space and develop a sense of common economic interest in both parts of the island'.[13] His contribution was well received by the business community and added to a growing demand for a greater degree of economic, if not political, co-operation.

As the year progressed Brooke concentrated on bringing the Northern politicians to the conference table, holding 'talks about talks' to overcome Unionist determination to do nothing while the Anglo-Irish Agreement continued to operate, though he was careful to emphasise that dialogue must also extend to the Dublin government. Others stressed the need for the Republic to repeal or alter Articles 2 and 3 of its Constitution (see above, p. 60). Brooke himself kept in close touch with the Republic's Foreign Minister, Gerry Collins, and facilitated regular Prime Ministerial meetings. Both Collins and the new leader of the Opposition, John Bruton, hinted at the possibility of altering the controversial Articles, though a motion to do so by the Workers Party, in the Dail in December 1990, was defeated by 74 votes to 66.

The Brooke initiative to create an inter-party dialogue within Northern Ireland, to be followed by dialogue between North and South, was the dominant Anglo-Irish political issue of 1990, the prospects of success waxing and waning amidst constant recriminations and attempts to secure preconditions. On 9 November a boost to the morale of change-seekers was given by the election of Mrs Mary Robinson as President of Ireland, though on the same day remarks by Brooke that Britain had no economic or strategic interest in remaining in Northern Ireland, and was therefore quite ready to accept Irish unification by consent, predictably caused irritation to Unionists. On 22 November top level change occurred in London, with Mrs Thatcher being forced to step down as Prime Minister, and on 27 November John Major emerged as her successor. Six days later, on 3 December, at her inauguration, President Robinson spoke of a 'new Ireland – open, tolerant and inclusive' and offered again to 'extend the hand of friendship' to the north.[14]

It was not until almost the end of March 1991 that the two main Unionist parties, plus the SDLP and Alliance, announced their acceptance of the latest formula devised by Peter Brooke to get constitutional talks started. 'A new and more broadly based agreement' would be sought, the patient Brooke explained, with focus being placed upon three relationships: 'those within Northern Ireland, including the relationship between any new institutions there and the Westminster parliament; among the people of the island of Ireland; and between the two governments'. Three strands of talks would reflect these relationships, the first concerning internal matters being followed before long (but on his judgement of the correct moment) by north–south talks, and then those between governments, all to be under way 'within weeks'. Nothing would be agreed until everything was agreed; the outcome would need to be 'acceptable to the people'.[15]

The talks did not proceed smoothly. The Unionist parties sought action from Dublin to remove the offensive Articles 2 and 3 of the Republic's Constitution, insisted that there be substantial progress on internal Northern Irish talks before a move was made to Strand Two, and then fought fiercely over the venue for talks in this second strand; the SDLP lost patience and announced it would not participate further until the government and the Unionists sorted out their differences; then disagreement arose over who was to be the independent chairman of the second strand. Meanwhile the ten-week gap in intergovernmental meetings of the Anglo-Irish Agreement, arranged to mollify Unionist sensitivities and to facilitate the talks, was fast expiring. On 14 June Sir Ninian Stephen, former Governor-General of Australia, was chosen as Strand Two Chairman, and on 17 June, after further squabbling, Sir Ninian was accepted, and talks under Strand One were started. Almost at once the Unionists warned that these would cease if the next scheduled Anglo-Irish Intergovernmental Meeting took place as planned on 16 July. Despite an increase in the pace of the talks, they in fact ceased on 3 July in the face of inflexibility in the Intergovernmental timetable. Recriminations and references to the possibility of resumption alternated intermittently for the rest of the year, but no new breakthrough occurred before Brooke's period as Secretary of State for Northern Ireland ended in April 1992.

8

CONCLUSION

Ireland has proved too small to be divided. Though their country was partitioned politically in 1920, the peoples of Ireland have rarely allowed this to interfere with daily life in practice. Even after seventy-five years of separate statehood they are, by and large, unwilling to regard as their stamping ground anything less than the whole island. During the war years, it is true, the political border assumed reality, and in recent decades the IRA campaign of violence has succeeded in deepening divisions and inhibiting movement. In general, however, the taking of holidays, the pursuit of leisure, and cultural and, increasingly, economic activities, simply ignore the political boundary.

God and Mammon are alike in this: the churches and banks equally preserve all-Ireland structures and coverage; and professional and academic associations and many sporting organisations and cultural and social bodies also dismiss the relevance of the political border. Dublin always attracted to its calendar of events visitors from north, south and beyond, not least to its International Horse Show each August, to its many concerts across the musical spectrum, to the All-Ireland Finals of the GAA and to International Rugby matches. Since 1964, Belfast has developed, through the initiative of Queen's University, an autumn Festival of music, theatre and the arts second only to that of Edinburgh, while the exhibitions of the Ulster Museum attract a wide attendance, and the Ulster Folk and Transport Museum provides a unique facility of European standard and all-Ireland significance. Throughout the island there is a plethora of summer events, often cultural and always social, that know no barriers: the Summer Schools of Yeats in Sligo and Hewitt in Ballycastle, the Waterford Light Opera

Festival, the Cork Film Festival or the new Folk, Drama and Arts events in Derry are but examples.

There are anomalies by the score. Despite being so small, Ireland boasts two national soccer teams, one or other of which has carried the admiration of most Irish fans, admitted or not, at the final stages of sucessive recent World Cups. Its single rugby team garners unstinting support from North and South in its international campaigns, and the same is true on a lesser scale for both men's and women's hockey and for cricket. The structure of Gaelic games is naturally island-wide and, in the hurling and football championships, the latter dominated by Ulster counties in recent years, pleasure at success is taken by many outside the natural constituency of the GAA.

Both parts of Ireland have produced poets and playwrights of international standing and novelists too, and sportsmen and soldiers of distinction, and many good citizens doing worthwhile jobs, rearing families with responsibility, attending to local needs, forming community groups and neighbourhood associations. Both have had their share also of thugs and vandals, of alienated young and of anti-social elements, not unlike modern Britain and indeed many countries in Europe where poverty and unemployment, exacerbated by racial, and in some cases religious, animosities, have led to destructive violence, isolated ghettoes, unsafe areas, dereliction and hopelessness.

The visitor to Ireland, North and South, will notice comparatively few examples of these latter trends. In the North, new housing schemes, a generous provision of leisure centres and sports fields, and major schemes such as the redevelopment of formerly neglected riversides in Belfast and Derry will catch the eye. In the South it is more likely to be the widespread rural presence of new bungalows and substantial houses that will attract attention. Throughout Ireland, the facilities for leisure, natural and built, for sailing and walking, fishing and riding, golfing and a variety of team sports, are well provided. As yet the environment is largely unpolluted, food ingredients are good, individuality, music, song, and convivial conversation remain widely appreciated. Irish people, on the whole, have retained their good humour, their generosity and their humanity, and, better educated, travelled and informed, they are notable, North and South, for their giving to the poor of the wider world. Weather permitting, the quality of life in Ireland itself can be high, without the requirement of a high income.

Less happily, severe unemployment is a feature in both parts of Ireland, and there are other trends to be deplored, too. Social workers, priests, teachers and commentators from a variety of perspectives regret the decline in religious values and discipline, a growth in crime, in marriage breakdown and in relationships outside marriage, in illegitimate births, in abortion, in drug abuse. Ireland as a whole remains a predominantly rural island, but in both parts the capital cities have grown to absorb around a third of all citizens, and in these centres, modern city problems are not absent. In this sense as in others, Ireland is part of Europe. And as a part of that Europe that has chosen to develop as one Community, the two Irelands, North and South, have been influenced substantially since entry in 1973.

Although the Republic of Ireland joined the EEC as a small, peripheral state with a largely agricultural economy, while Northern Ireland entered at the same moment as part of a major player on the world stage, a region of the United Kingdom, a largely, though declining, industrial state, the two Irelands shared many characteristics, more indeed than at the time of partition, and their experience of Europe since has tended to reinforce what they hold in common. In this context, as will be seen, some of the earlier recorded characteristics of Belfast–Dublin relations have been reversed.

In 1920, Northern Ireland came into being containing the substantial proportion of the island's industry. When, a year later, the Irish Free State was conceived, it was to embrace a territory overwhelmingly agricultural. Economic shifts and vicissitudes had changed much by 1973, and the future was to confirm the position: oil crises in that year and in 1979, together with other economic trends, were to enhance both the industrial decimation of the North and the slow growth of industry to supremacy over agriculture in the Republic. It was thus that, at the moment of their entry to the European Community, by agreement on 22 January 1972, to come into effect on 1 January 1973, the two parts of Ireland had much more in common than at the time of their separation.

Of course it must be born in mind that, being independent, the Republic enjoyed a budgetary autonomy lacking in Northern Ireland, that two different currencies obtained (more significant after 1979 when the Irish pound broke with sterling upon entry into the European Monetary System), that different fiscal arrangements influenced taxation and public expenditure decisions and that wage determination, too, was direct in the Republic but dictated by UK mechanisms in Northern Ireland.[1]

Nevertheless, it has been remarked that the independent Irish economy and the Northern Irish region of the UK economy were alike in being 'relatively "open" by virtue of size, limited home market, resource endowment, location and policy strategy'; that they were at 'broadly similar stages of development'; that they 'shared close commercial, trading and cultural links with Britain', and that their labour markets were also linked to that country; that both suffered higher unemployment rates than were general in the EEC; and that agriculture, fishing and forestry accounted for a more significant proportion of employment and economic activity than was general in the rest of the Market. Furthermore, they shared also the disadvantages of peripheral location, high birth rates, with consequent needs for job-creation, and low population densities (the Republic's being more than twice as low as that of Northern Ireland). Both also experienced (and the experience was to increase rather than diminish) high reliance on public-sector employment, budgetary pressures from high dependency rates, and the need for 'substantial resource transfers from outside'.[2] How did these two economic regions fare within the new European context and how did their common membership impinge on their mutual relationships?

Recent historical accounts[3] have been careful to add an element of self-inflicted damage to the locational and structural disadvantages and the external blows suffered by the two Irelands in the 1970s and 1980s: economic misman-agement in the case of the Republic; inter-communal violence in that of the North. In a characteristically hard-hitting analysis of the Republic, Professor J. J. Lee pointed out that the uncompetitive nature of Irish industry was already becoming apparent within the limited British context by the time of EEC entry and that Irish Ministers looked rather to the likelihood of huge agricultural gains to be reaped from higher European prices, as well as from the subsidies likely to flow to a peripheral region following membership, than to industrial competitiveness. To those who feared the undermining of Irish sovereignty, the 1972 Irish White Paper on accession made it clear that a small country such as Ireland had no real freedom to take national action in the economic and trading sectors so that its interest could best be served by gaining at least a voice in the European decision-making process.[4]

But if the decision to bid for Europe was one of the highlights of 1972, that year marked also a departure from good housekeeping by the Republic's Fianna Fail government, as Finance Minister Colley moved to embrace deficit budgeting, and the start of a slide into economic unreality. Short-term, political expedients were to lead in the future to more and more borrowing to sustain a standard of living to which the Irish were glad to become accustomed but which they showed no signs of being able to earn. The end of the decade, however, saw the dramatic reckoning, with wage and inflation rates well above EEC average levels and dramatic increases in unemployment and foreign debt: wages in 1981 up 18.4% (about the average from 1978) with the EEC 11.6% (again about the average from 1978); inflation at 20.4%, compared with 7.6% in 1978 (EEC up from 7.4% to 11.6%); unemployment standing in 1981 at 147,000, compared with 98,367 in 1978,[5] and foreign debt up from £297m in the former year to £3,451m in the latter. (As recently as 1973, Ireland had been a creditor country.) It was to deteriorate to

£5,114m in 1982 before the new Coalition Government of Garret FitzGerald began to restore confidence and good practice, but the rising trend proved impossible to curb even then.

Agricultural incomes did increase considerably for a time, and by 1978 had probably doubled in real terms since 1970.[6] The following year brought a cold draft however, as the Common Agricultural Policy began more realistic pricing in the face of mounting food surpluses. Unrealistically high Irish land prices began to fall, and those who had borrowed on land had their debts called in. Family farm incomes fell steadily, and net receipts from the EEC, up from £104m in 1976 to £448m in 1979, levelled to £457m in 1980 before falling to £387m in 1981. A more depressed decade of the 1980s began, presaged in 1979 by the entry of the Republic into the EMS, the second international oil crisis and the accession to power of Charles Haughey in December, all of which ushered in the new era.

Haughey could recognise that 'as a community we are living away beyond our means . . . we are living at a rate which is simply not justified by the amount of goods and services we are producing,[7] but immediate electoral imperatives prevented him from applying the required corrective restraints. Budget deficits rose (£802m in 1981; £988 in 1982) and government expenditure as a percentage of GNP reached a staggering 66.9% in 1982 (48.8% in 1977).

It fell to Garret FitzGerald's Fine Gael, in partnership once more with Labour, now led by Dick Spring, to 'pick up the pieces'.[8] Returning to power in November 1982 (he had briefly been Coalition Taoiseach from June 1981 to March 1982), FitzGerald succeeded, in the years to the next election in March 1987, in restoring a semblance of respectability to the Republic's economy, and indeed to a political system that had begun to show signs of deep party-political penetration. Increases in taxation and in non-tax income and cuts in expenditure started the economic recovery; patent concern to restore civil service and police standards uncontaminated by political pressures as well as an energetic pursuit of Public

Service reform helped these vital institutions of state back to apolitical neutrality.

One measure of economic rectitude was the reduction of the inflation rate to below 5% by 1987, and it was to fall to 3.5% by 1990, but unemployment at the end of the 1980s hovered around 18%, and the debt burden, while showing some stability, had grown in both foreign and domestic sectors, the former standing at IR£8.8bn, the latter IR£16.2bn (i.e. a total over IR£25bn) in 1990.

The 1980s were also FitzGerald's busy years of constitutional crusading, of summit meetings with Prime Minister Thatcher, of the New Ireland Forum and the 1985 Anglo-Irish Agreement, as outlined in Chapter 7 above: courageous and sensitive attempts on the one hand 'to contemplate the implications for Protestants of a Catholic parliament for a Catholic people' (a challenge posed to nationalist Ireland in the seventies, almost single-handedly by Dr Conor Cruise O'Brien),[9] and on the other to underpin faith in democratic institutions, North and South, and to drive out from both the influence of violent men.

During the 1970s and 1980s the structure of the Irish economy also altered, with a steady decline of agriculture as a percentage of GDP, from 16% in 1971 to 10% in 1990 (the EEC average in 1989 being 3%), while industry fell slightly from 36% to 35% in the same period (EEC 33% in 1989), services moving up from 48% to 55% (EEC 64% in 1989). In Northern Ireland agriculture dropped from 7% in 1971 to 4% in 1990, industry from 40% to 28%, and services rose from 53% to 68%.[10]

These latter comparisons show similar trends, at different levels, but mask the devastation of the industrial sector in the North. The second international oil crisis, added to the continuing political disturbance in the province, proved sufficient in the 1979–81 period to close down 110 substantial manufacturing firms there.[11] By July 1982 unemployment had reached 21.1% of the insured working population, and although this figure dropped back, to average between 17% and 18% in the rest of the 1980s, the province moved closer to

mic profile of its rural Southern neighbour. Within
ean Community this was to be a significant factor, as
ations of the Single European Act (1987) and its
Single Market (end of 1992) became apparent.

Along with economic stagnation, the political situation in
Northern Ireland stabilised in the 1980s into an uneasy
balance under direct Westminster rule. The outraged Unionist
reaction to the 1985 Anglo-Irish Agreement achieved little,
violence continued at a 'contained' level, and for most people
life went on in what had become a normal manner. Strenuous
but quiet and undemonstrative efforts were made at many
levels and under government and private initiatives to
promote tolerance and neighbourliness amongst communities
that had at times been traumatised by atrocity and murderous
cruelty.

The lead was given within the education system in the early
eighties with the clear responsibility being laid upon schools
to provide eduation for mutual understanding, a concept
(EMU) since developed with sensitivity and imagination. At
the same time parents, dissatisfied with the all-too-rigid
division of the education system into Protestant (State) and
Catholic (Voluntary) sectors, began a campaign for integrated
education. The first integrated secondary school, Lagan
College, was begun in 1981, and a decade later some sixteen
integrated primary and secondary schools had been both
established and brought within the aegis of the Department
of Education. By that time, too, the adoption of a national
curriculum had laid further duties upon all schools through
cross-curricular themes, not only in EMU but in Cultural
Heritage, the latter reflecting considerable work, undertaken
with government support, to stress to the peoples of the
province the mutual enrichment to be found in their
contrasting cultural traditions, in music, sport, language and
literature, hitherto viewed more as threat than opportunity.

This work preceded the founding in 1990 of a Community
Relations Commission (CRC), itself the result of trends
nurtured by the small, pioneering Central Community
Relations Unit, established by government in 1987. It was the

responsibility of CRC to assist the many voluntary bodies (e.g. Protestant and Catholic Encounter, Women Together, the Corrymeela Community, Co-operation North) already working in the field but short of resources and professional expertise, and to take initiatives of its own to promote awareness and understanding and reduce prejudice and fear. Slow to produce results, these moves epitomise the less publicised side of life in Northern Ireland. Their hard won experience has made its mark for the better on the province; it may yet turn out to be relevant in other parts of the modern world, not least in Eastern Europe, where new conflicts of allegiance and national sovereignty have begun to exhibit the worst features of inhumanity and destructiveness.

Co-operation North, the brainchild of Brendan O'Regan, former boss of the Shannon Development Scheme and of Bord Failte, the Irish Republic's Tourism Board, is distinct from other bodies operating in the North in originating in the South. It was specifically formed on the principle that economic co-operation and contacts between the two parts of Ireland could only be of mutual benefit and must in time reduce fear and erode violence. It chimed closely with what the European Community was creating in practice as the eighties gave way to the nineties: a context in which borders became increasingly meaningless and where inter-state co-operation would reap disproportionate benefit; a context where some traditional attitudes and perspectives could be confounded.

Which brings this account finally to some of the paradoxes of the new Europe. It has long been the case that the three MEPs from Northern Ireland, representing competing SDLP, DUP and OUP constituents, have found it possible to work harmoniously together in Brussels and Strasbourg when the interests of the province are at stake. It has also been the case that as the two parts of Ireland have come to resemble one another, leaving Northern Ireland with rather different priorities than the United Kingdom as a whole, so Dublin has often argued for European measures more to Belfast's liking than those proposed by London. It is through Westminster that Belfast's wishes must be directed, however, and this is no easy process, so the direct access that Dublin enjoys as an independent state member of the Community is often the envy of Northern businessmen and farmers.

What was perhaps less well known until the autobiography of a concerned ex-Taoiseach was published, is just how often Dublin itself has intervened by its own initiative, on Belfast's behalf. Given a sense of responsibility for the well-being of all the island's citizens, that is not so surprising, perhaps, though it is fairly clear that it took a Fine Gael-dominated Coalition Government and an unusual individual at the helm to produce action.

As early as 1969 Garret FitzGerald, turning his career towards politics, had drafted Fine Gael's policy in regard to Irish unity, insisting that 'the only way in which the present divided state of this island can, or should be modified is with the consent of a majority of the people of Northern Ireland'.[12] He did not waver from this conviction in the future, taking trouble when Foreign Minister, 1973–7, to stress to London that Dublin would not accept Northern Ireland as a gift, that Dublin saw London's continued management of Northern affairs as vital in the foreseeable future, if economic and political stability were to survive. FitzGerald clearly regretted, from time to time (most notably during the Ulster Workers Strike of 1974, that brought down Faulkner's power-sharing executive), that London did not seem as able to understand the realities on the ground in Belfast as did observers in Dublin; and that conflicts of interpretation between separate elements of the British state machine (the Northern Ireland Office, the Foreign Office and even the Cabinet Office) could lead to confused and at times harmful action.[13]

While Taoiseach he found London was unconvinced that he could remove by referendum Articles 2 and 3 of his country's Constitution: Articles offensive to Ulster Unionists and which he was proposing to tackle.[14] Though aspiring to woo all Northerners to join the Irish state, he had long realised that constitutional changes would be required if the unity dream was ever to be fulfilled, and his objectives in office were consistently to remove the fears of Unionists, gain recognition for the rights of Northern nationalists, and undermine the forces of violence. While so doing he welcomed European initiatives to develop the economy of the North as well as the South, and so stimulate the jobs which could reduce idleness and frustration, the parents of violent action. At least some Unionists may have realised that they had something of a friend in office in Dublin, one whom many had met personally, for FitzGerald had Northern roots and kept up his contacts. There was further paradox in his use of his European influence to convince other Community leaders to treat exceptionally the problems of Northern Ireland, an example being his persuasion of President Mitterrand, in November 1981, to withdraw French objection to the use of Community funds for housing in the province.[15]

Behind his attitude, as FitzGerald himself had stressed in the mid-seventies, was the assumption that it was for the future to decide on Irish unity, that for the time being his government 'favoured self-government within the United Kingdom'[16] for the province, if only an equitable form of self-government could be agreed. His work stands out, not mirrored visibly by his political opponents who have monopolised office, but it remains an example of how better Belfast–Dublin accord might be achieved. In the meantime, it has to be said, there is still lacking in the nineties any willingness amongst the Northern majority to give allegiance to a Dublin regime.

In an account of his Southern fellow citizens, the Northern-born Professor of English at Trinity College Dublin, Terence Brown, complained in 1981 of the middle classes, at least those 'in the towns and cities', that they had not lived up to the civilising and Christianising hopes of those who had fought against the former imperial yoke, but rather 'were content to live a comfortable, petit-bourgeois life that bore a closer relationship to the life of similarly placed people in Britain than to any vision of special destiny'.[17] The same might then have been said of his former compatriots north of the border. In the nineteen-nineties the denizens of Dublin and Belfast might both be thought a little livelier, a little more aware, a little more ambitious materially, fitting a little less the English stereotype. But in the North still, and in the South perhaps more so, both seem content enough to go their separate political ways. Both their decisions may have been influenced by the bloody activities of the Irish Republican Army. It remains to be seen whether or not its cessation of military action,[18] if adhered to, will permit the long healing process necessary for reconciliation to begin, and whether, after that, the 'generosity and imagination', called for by the former Taoiseach, Garret FitzGerald, from both sides, can 'eventually bring the people of this island together in a full partnership'.[19]

APPENDIX A

EXTRACTS FROM THE GOVERNMENT OF IRELAND ACT, 1920

Government of Ireland Act, 1920

[Introduced into the House of Commons, 25 February, received the royal assent 23 December 1920.]

An Act to provide for the better government of Ireland

Be it enacted . . .

1. (1) On and after the appointed day[1] there shall be established for Southern Ireland a parliament to be called the parliament of Southern Ireland consisting of his majesty, the senate of Southern Ireland, and the house of commons of Southern Ireland, and there shall be established for Northern Ireland a parliament to be called the parliament of Northern Ireland consisting of his majesty, the senate of Northern Ireland, and the house of commons of Northern Ireland.

(2) For the purposes of this act, Northern Ireland shall consist of the parliamentary counties of Antrim, Armagh, Down, Fermanagh, Londonderry and Tyrone, and the parliamentary boroughs of Belfast and Londonderry, and Southern Ireland shall consist of so much of Ireland as is not comprised within the said parliamentary counties and boroughs.

---

[1] A date not later than fifteen months after the passing of the act, to be fixed by order in council.

2. (1) With a view to the eventual establishment of a parliament for the whole of Ireland, and to bringing about harmonious action between the parliaments and governments of Southern Ireland and Northern Ireland, and to the promotion of mutual intercourse and uniformity in relation to matters affecting the whole of Ireland, and to providing for the administration of services which the two parliaments mutually agree should be administered uniformly throughout the whole of Ireland, or which by virtue of this act are to be so administered, there shall be constituted, as soon as may be after the appointed day, a council to be called the council of Ireland.

(2) Subject as hereinafter provided, the council of Ireland shall consist of a person nominated by the lord lieutenant acting in accordance with instructions from his majesty who shall be president, and forty other persons, of whom seven shall be members of the senate of Southern Ireland, thirteen shall be members of the house of commons of Southern Ireland, seven shall be members of the senate of Northern Ireland, and thirteen shall be members of the house of commons of Northern Ireland.

The members of the council of Ireland shall be elected in each case by the members of that house of the parliament of Southern Ireland or Northern Ireland of which they are members . . .

(3) The constitution of the council of Ireland may from time to time be varied by identical acts passed by the parliament of Southern Ireland and the parliament of Northern Ireland, and the acts may provide for all or any of the members of the council of Ireland being elected by parliamentary electors, . . .

3. (1) The parliaments of Southern Ireland and Northern Ireland may, by identical acts agreed to by an absolute majority of members of the house of commons of each parliament at the third reading (hereinafter referred to as constituent acts), establish, in lieu of the council of Ireland, a parliament for the whole of Ireland consisting of his majesty and two houses. . . .

(2) On the date of Irish union the council of Ireland shall cease to exist and there shall be transferred to the parliament and government of Ireland all powers then exercisable by the council of Ireland, . . .

(3) There shall also be transferred to the parliament and government of Ireland, except so far as the constituent acts otherwise provide, all the powers and duties of the parliaments and governments of Southern Ireland and Northern Ireland. . . .

4. (1) Subject to the provisions of this act, the parliament of Southern Ireland and the parliament of Northern Ireland shall respectively have power to make laws for the peace, order, and good government of Southern Ireland and Northern Ireland with the following limitations, namely, that they shall not have power to make laws except in respect of matters exclusively relating to the portion of Ireland within their jurisdiction, or some part thereof, and (without prejudice to that general limitation) that they shall not have power to make laws in respect of the following matters in particular, namely: [here follows the substance of clause 2 of the Government of Ireland Act, 1914].

6. (1) Neither the parliament of Southern Ireland nor the parliament of Northern Ireland shall have power to repeal or alter any provision of this act (except as is specially provided by this act), or of any act passed by the parliament of the United Kingdom after the appointed day and extending to the part of Ireland within their jurisdiction, . . .

7. (1) The council of Ireland shall have power to make orders with respect to matters affecting interests both in Southern Ireland and Northern Ireland, in any case where the matter –

    (*a*)   Is of such a nature that if it had affected interests in one of those areas only it would have been within the powers of the parliament for that area: and

    (*b*)   Is a matter to affect which, it would apart from this provision, have been necessary to apply to the parliament of the United Kingdom by petition for leave to bring in a private bill.

8. (2) As respects Irish services, the lord lieutenant . . . shall exercise any prerogative or other executive power of his majesty, the exercise of which may be delegated to him by his majesty: . . .

(3) Subject to the provisions of this act relating to the council of Ireland, powers so delegated shall be exercised –

(*a*) In Southern Ireland, through such departments as may be established by act of the parliament of Southern Ireland, or, subject to any alteration by act of that parliament, by the lord lieutenant: and

(*b*) In Northern Ireland, through such departments as may be established by act of the parliament of Northern Ireland, or, subject to any alteration by act of that parliament, by the lord lieutenant: and the lord lieutenant may appoint officers to administer those departments, and those officers shall hold office during the pleasure of the lord lieutenant.

9. (1) The Royal Irish Constabulary and the Dublin Metropolitan Police . . . shall be reserved matters until such date, not being later than the expiration of three years after the appointed day as his majesty in council may determine . . .

(2) The following matters, namely:

(*a*) the postal service; (*b*) the Post Office Savings Bank and Trustee Savings Bank; (*c*) designs for stamps, whether for postal or revenue purposes; (*d*) the registration of deeds and the Public Record Office of Ireland; shall be reserved matters until the date of Irish union, . . . and on that date if there should be no provision to the contrary in the constituent acts . . . the public services in connexion with the administration of those matters, except in so far as they are matters with respect to which the parliament of Ireland have not power to make laws, shall, by virtue of this act, be transferred from the government of the United Kingdom to the government of Ireland, . . .

10. (1) The parliaments of Southern Ireland and Northern Ireland may, by identical acts, delegate to the council of Ireland any of the powers of the parliaments and governments of Southern Ireland and Northern Ireland, and such acts may determine the manner in which the powers so delegated are to be exercisable by the council.

(2) With a view to the uniform administration throughout Ireland . . . any powers (not being powers relating to reserved matters) exercisable by any department of the government of the United Kingdom at the appointed day with respect to railways and fisheries and the contagious diseases of animals in Ireland and the power of making laws with respect to railways and fisheries and the contagious diseases of animals shall, as from the appointed day, become powers of the council of Ireland, . . .

(3) The council may consider any questions which may appear in any way to bear on the welfare of both Southern Ireland and Northern Ireland, and may, by resolution, make suggestions in relation thereto as they may think proper, but suggestions so made shall have no legislative effect, . . .

12. The lord lieutenant shall give and withhold the assent of his majesty to bills passed by the senate and house of commons of Southern Ireland or the senate and house of commons of Northern Ireland, and to orders of the council of Ireland, subject to the following limitations:

(1) He shall comply with any instructions given by his majesty in respect of any such bill or order; and

(2) He shall, if so directed by his majesty, reserve any such bill or order for the signification of his majesty's pleasure, . . .

19. Unless and until the parliament of the United Kingdom otherwise determine, . . . the number of members to be returned by constituencies in Ireland to serve in the parliament of the United Kingdom shall be forty-six, . . .

20. (1) There shall be an exchequer and consolidated fund of Southern Ireland and an exchequer and consolidated fund of

Northern Ireland separate from one another and from those of the United Kingdom.

21. (1) The power of the parliaments of Southern Ireland and Northern Ireland to make laws shall include power to make laws with respect to the imposing, charging, levying, and collection of taxes within their respective jurisdictions, other than customs duties, excise duties on articles manufactured and produced, and excess profits duty, corporation profits tax, and any other tax on profits, and (except to the extent hereinafter mentioned) income tax (including super-tax), or any tax substantially the same in character as any of those duties or taxes, . . .

22. (1) The imposing, charging, levying, and collection of customs duties and of excise duties on articles manufactured and produced and the granting of customs and excise drawbacks and allowances, and, except to the extent here-inafter mentioned, the imposing, charging, levying, and collection of income tax (including super-tax) and excess profits duty, corporation profits tax, and any other tax on profits shall be reserved matters, and the proceeds of those duties and taxes shall be paid into the consolidated fund of the United Kingdom.

(2) The joint exchequer board shall in each year determine what part of the proceeds of the said duties and taxes . . . are properly attributed to Ireland . . . and the sum so determined to be the Irish share of the proceeds of the said duties and taxes is hereinafter referred to as the Irish share of reserved taxes.

23. (1) Ireland shall in each year make a contribution towards the imperial liabilities and expenditure . . .

(3) The proportion of imperial liabilities and expenditure to be so contributed shall be such as the joint exchequer board may . . . determine to be just; . . .

(4) The said contribution shall be apportioned as between Southern Ireland and Northern Ireland in the following manner, that is to say:

(*a*) So long as the contribution remains at the rate of eighteen million pounds a year, fifty-six per centum thereof shall be apportioned to Southern Ireland and forty-four per centum thereof to Northern Ireland:

(*b*) Thereafter such part shall be apportioned to Southern Ireland and Northern Ireland respectively as the joint exchequer board may determine to correspond to their relative taxable capacities . . .

24. (1) There shall in respect of each year be charged on and paid out of the consolidated fund of the United Kingdom to the exchequers of Southern Ireland and Northern Ireland a sum equal to the Irish share of reserved taxes in that year after deducting –

(*a*) the amount of the Irish contribution towards imperial liabilities and expenditure; and

(*b*) whilst any services remain reserved services, the net cost to the exchequer of the United Kingdom during the year of the services . . .

(3) In determining the apportionment as between the exchequers of Southern and Northern Ireland of the Irish residuary share of reserved taxes, the joint exchequer board shall act on the following principles:

(*a*) So far as the amount of the said share depends on the proceeds of any tax, they shall determine what parts of the proceeds are properly attribute to Southern and Northern Ireland respectively, and shall allot the amount so determined accordingly:

(*b*) So far as the amount of the said share depends on the amount of the Irish contribution towards imperial liabilities and expenditure, they shall allot to Southern Ireland and Northern Ireland their respective shares in that contribution determined in manner hereinbefore provided.

(*c*) So far as the amount of the said share depends on the cost of any service, they shall, where the cost of the service in Southern and Northern Ireland respectively can be ascertained, allot to Southern and Northern Ireland the cost of the service in Southern and Northern Ireland respectively; and where the cost of the service in Southern and Northern Ireland cannot in their opinion be ascertained with sufficient accuracy, they shall divide the cost between them in proportion to population.

26. (1) Purchase annuities payable in respect of land situate in Southern Ireland and Northern Ireland respectively, including any arrears thereof due to accruing due on the appointed day, shall be collected by the governments of Southern Ireland and Northern Ireland, and the amounts so collected shall be paid into their respective exchequers, but nothing in this act shall confer on either such government any powers with respect to the redemption of purchase annuities.

32. (1) For the purposes of the financial provisions of this act, there shall be established a board to be called the joint exchequer board, consisting of two members appointed by the treasury, one member appointed by the treasury of Southern Ireland, one member appointed by the treasury of Northern Ireland, and a chairman appointed by his majesty.

38. The supreme court of judicature in Ireland shall cease to exist, and there shall be established in Ireland the following courts, that is to say, a court having jurisdiction in Southern Ireland, to be called the supreme court of judicature of Southern Ireland, a court having jurisdiction in Northern Ireland, to be called the supreme court of judicature in Northern Ireland, and a court having appellate jurisdiction throughout the whole of Ireland, to be called the High court of appeal for Ireland.

43. (1) An appeal shall lie to the high court of appeal for Ireland from any decision of the court of appeal in Southern Ireland or the court of appeal in Northern Ireland, and all questions which under the *Crown cases act*, 1848, would be reserved for the decision of the judges of the high court shall be reserved for the decision of the high court of appeal for

Ireland, whose decision shall, except as hereinafter provided, be final, . . .

49. An appeal shall lie from the high court of appeal for Ireland to the house of lords –

(*a*)   in any case where under existing enactments such an appeal would lie from the existing court of appeal in Ireland to the house of lords;

(*b*)   in any case where a person is aggrieved by any decision of the high court of appeal for Ireland in any proceedings taken by way of certiorari, mandamus, quo warranto or prohibition;

(*c*)   in any case where a decision of the high court of appeal for Ireland involves a decision of any question as to the validity of any law made by or having the effect of an act of the parliament of Southern Ireland or Northern Ireland . . .

51. If it appears to the lord lieutenant or a secretary of state expedient in the public interest that steps shall be taken for the speedy determination of the question whether any act, or order having the effect of an act of the parliament of Southern Ireland or Northern Ireland, or any provision thereof, or any bill introduced in either of those parliaments, or any provision thereof or any legislative proposal before the council of Ireland, is beyond the powers of such parliament or council, whether any service is an Irish service within the meaning of this act or not, or if the joint exchequer board, or any two members of the board, in the execution of their duties under this act, are desirous of obtaining the decision of any question of the interpretation of this act, or other question of law, which arises in connexion with those duties, the lord lieutenant, secretary of state, or board, or members thereof, as the case may be, may represent the same to his majesty in council, and thereupon, if his majesty so directs, the said question shall be forthwith referred to and heard and determined by the judicial committee of the privy council.

75. Notwithstanding the establishment of the Parliaments of Southern and Northern Ireland, or the Parliament of Ireland, or anything contained in this Act, the supreme authority of the Parliament of the United Kingdom shall remain unaffected and undiminished over all persons, matters and things in Ireland and any part thereof.

76. (1) This Act may be cited as the Government of Ireland Act, 1920.

2 The Government of Ireland Act, 1914, is hereby repealed as from the passing of this Act.

10 and 11 Geo. V, cap. 67.

Appendix B

Articles of Agreement for a Treaty between Great Britain and Ireland, 1921

34. ARTICLES OF AGREEMENT FOR A TREATY BETWEEN GREAT BRITAIN AND IRELAND, DATED THE SIXTH DAY OF DECEMBER 1921

1. Ireland shall have the same constitutional status in the community of nations known as the British Empire as the Dominion of Canada, the Commonwealth of Australia, the Dominion of New Zealand, and the Union of South Africa, with a parliament having powers to make laws for the peace and good government of Ireland and an executive responsible to that parliament, and shall be styled and known as the Irish Free State.

2. Subject to the provisions hereinafter set out the position of the Irish Free State in relation to the imperial parliament and government and otherwise shall be that of the Dominion of Canada, and the law, practice and constitutional usage governing and relationship of the crown or the representative of the crown and of the imperial parliament to the Dominion of Canada shall govern their relationship to the Irish Free State.

3. The representative of the crown in Ireland shall be appointed in like manner as the governor-general of Canada, and in accordance with the practice observed in making of such appointments.

4. The oath to be taken by members of the parliament of the Irish Free State shall be in the following form: I —— do solemnly swear true faith and allegiance to the constitution of the Irish Free State as by law established and that I will be faithful to H. M. King George V, his heirs and successors by law in virtue of the common citizenship of Ireland with Great Britain and her adherence to and membership of the group of nations forming the British Commonwealth of nations.

5. The Irish Free State shall assume liability for the service of the public debt of the United Kingdom as existing at the date hereof and towards the payment of war pensions as existing at that date in such proportion as may be fair and equitable, having regard to any just claims on the part of Ireland by way of set off or counter-claim, the amount of such sums being determined in default of agreement by the arbitration of one or more independent persons being citizens of the British empire.

6. Until an arrangement has been made between the British and Irish governments whereby the Irish Free State under-takes her own coastal defence, the defence by sea of Great Britain and Ireland shall be undertaken by his majesty's imperial forces, but this shall not prevent the construction or maintenance by the government of the Irish Free State of such vessels as are necessary for the protection of the revenue or the fisheries.

The foregoing provisions of this article shall be reviewed at a conference of representatives of the British and Irish govern-ments to be held at the expiration of five years from the date hereof with a view to the undertaking by Ireland of a share in her own coastal defence.

7. The government of the Irish Free State shall afford to his majesty's imperial forces:

(*a*) In time of peace such harbour and other facilities as are indicated in the annex hereto, or such other facilities as may from time to time be agreed between the British government and the government of the Irish Free State; and

(*b*) In time of war or of strained relations with a foreign power such harbour and other facilities as the British government may require for the purposes of such defence as aforesaid.

8. With a view to securing the observance of the principle of international limitation of armaments, if the government of the Irish Free State establishes and maintains a military defence force, the establishments thereof shall not exceed in size such proportion of the military establishments maintained in Great Britain as that which the population of Ireland bears to the population of Great Britain.

9. The ports of Great Britain and the Irish Free State shall be freely open to the ships of the other country on payment of the customary port and other dues.

10. The government of the Irish Free State agrees to pay fair compensation on terms not less favourable than those accorded by the act of 1920 to judges, officials, members of police forces, and other public servants who are discharged by it or who retire in consequence of the change of government effected in pursuance hereof.

Provided that this agreement shall not apply to members of the Auxiliary Police Force or to persons recruited in Great Britain for the Royal Irish Constabulary during the two years next preceding the date hereof. The British government will assume responsibility for such compensation or pensions as may be payable to any of these excepted persons.

11. Until the expiration of one month from the passing of the act of parliament for the ratification of this instrument, the powers of the parliament and the government of the Irish Free State shall not be exercisable as respects Northern Ireland, and the provisions of the *Government of Ireland Act,* 1920, shall, so far as they relate to Northern Ireland, remain of full force and effect, and no election shall be held for the return of members to serve in the parliament of the Irish Free State for constituencies in Northern Ireland, unless a resolution is passed by both houses of the parliament of Northern Ireland in favour of the holding of such elections before the end of the said month.

12. If before the expiration of the said month, an address is presented to his majesty by both houses of the parliament of Northern Ireland to that effect, the powers of the parliament and government of the Irish Free State shall no longer extend to Northern Ireland, and the provisions of the *Government of Ireland Act,* 1920 (including those relating to the council of Ireland), shall so far as they relate to Northern Ireland, continue to be of full force and effect, and this instrument shall have effect subject to the necessary modifications.

Provided that if such an address is so presented a commission consisting of three persons, one to be appointed by the government of the Irish Free State, one to be appointed by the government of Northern Ireland, and one who shall be chairman to be appointed by the British government shall determine in accordance with the wishes of the inhabitants, so far as may be compatible with economic and geographic conditions, the boundaries between Northern Ireland and the rest of Ireland, and for the purposes of the *Government of Ireland Act,* 1920 and of this instrument, the boundary of Northern Ireland shall be such as may be determined by such commission.

13. For the purpose of the last foregoing article, the powers of the parliament of Southern Ireland under the *Government of Ireland Act,* 1920, to elect members of the council of Ireland

shall after the parliament of the Irish Free State is constituted be exercised by that parliament.

14. After the expiration of the said month, if no such address as is mentioned in article 12 hereof is presented, the parliament and government of Northern Ireland shall continue to exercise as respects Northern Ireland the powers conferred on them by the *Government of Ireland Act*, 1920, but the parliament and government of the Irish Free State shall in Northern Ireland have in relation to matters in respect of which the parliament of Northern Ireland has not the power to make laws under that act (including matters which under the said act are within the jurisdiction of the council of Ireland) the same powers as in the rest of Ireland, subject to such other provisions as may be agreed in manner hereinafter appearing.

15. At any time after the date hereof the government of Northern Ireland and the provisional government of Southern Ireland hereinafter constituted may meet for the purpose of discussing the provisions subject to which the last foregoing article is to operate in the event of no such address as is therein mentioned being presented, and those provisions may include:

(*a*) Safeguards with regard to patronage in Northern Ireland.
(*b*) Safeguards with regard to the collection of revenue in Northern Ireland.
(*c*) Safeguards with regard to import and export duties affecting the trade or industry of Northern Ireland.
(*d*) Safeguard for minorities in Northern Ireland.
(*e*) The settlement of the financial relations between Northern Ireland and the Irish Free State.
(*f*) The establishment and powers of a local militia in Northern Ireland and the relation of the defence forces of the Irish Free State and of Northern Ireland respectively,

and if at any such meeting provisions are agreed to, the same shall have effect as if they were included amongst the provisions subject to which the powers of the parliament and government of the Irish Free State are to be exercisable in Northern Ireland under Article 14 hereof.

16. Neither the parliament of the Irish Free State nor the parliament of Northern Ireland shall make any law so as either directly or indirectly to endow any religion or prohibit or restrict the free exercise thereof or give any preference or impose any disability on account of religious belief or religious status or affect prejudicially the right of any child to attend a school receiving public money without attending the religious instruction at the school or make any discrimination as respects state aid between schools under the management of different religious denominations or divert from any religious denomination or any educational institution any of its property except for public utility purposes and on payment of compensation.

17. By way of provisional arrangement for the administration of Southern Ireland during the interval which must elapse between the date hereof and the constitution of a parliament and government in accordance therewith, steps shall be taken forthwith for summoning a meeting of members of parliament elected for constituencies in Southern Ireland since the passing of the *Government of Ireland Act*, 1920, and for constituting a provisional government, and the British government shall take the steps necessary to transfer to such provisional government the powers and machinery requisite for the discharge of its duties, provided that every member of such provisional government shall have signified in writing his or her acceptance of this instrument. But this arrangement shall not continue in force beyond the expiration of twelve months from the date hereof.

18. This instrument shall be submitted forthwith by his majesty's government for the approval of parliament and by

the Irish signatories to a meeting summoned for the purpose of the members elected to sit in the house of commons of Southern Ireland, and if approved shall be ratified by the necessary legislation

(*Signed*)
On behalf of the British
  Delegation,

D. Lloyd George
Austen Chamberlain
Birkenhead
Winston S. Churchill
L. Worthington-Evans
Hamar Greenwood
Gordon Hewart

On behalf of the Irish
  Delegation,

Art O. Gríobhtha (Arthur
  Griffith)
Mícheál O. Coileáin
Riobárd Bartún
Eudhmenn S. O. Dugáin
Seórsa Ghabháin Uí
  Dhubhthaigh

6th December 1921

Saorstat Éireann, public general acts, 1922, pp. 44–8.

[The Annex appended to this Act included the provision of naval facilities at Berehaven, Queenstown, Belfast Lough and Lough Swilly.]

APPENDIX C(1)

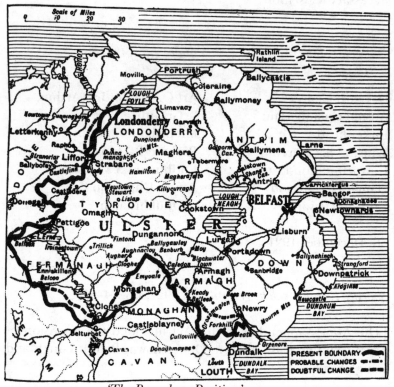

'The Boundary Position'

Map printed in the *Morning Post*, 7 November 1925.

IRELAND (CONFIRMATION OF AGREEMENT) ACT, 1925

Schedule

AGREEMENT AMENDING AND SUPPLEMENTING THE ARTICLES OF AGREEMENT FOR A TREATY BETWEEN GREAT BRITAIN AND IRELAND TO WHICH THE FORCE OF LAW WAS GIVEN BY THE IRISH FREE STATE (AGREEMENT) ACT, 1922, AND BY THE CONSTITUTION OF THE IRISH FREE STATE (SAORSTAT EIREANN) ACT, 1922

Whereas on the sixth day of December nineteen hundred and twenty-one Articles of Agreement for a Treaty between Great Britain and Ireland were entered into:

And whereas the said Articles of Agreement were duly ratified and given the force of law by the Irish Free State (Agreement) Act, 1992, and by the Constitution of the Irish Free State (Saorstat Fireann) Act, 1992:

And whereas the progress of events and the improved relations now subsisting between the British Government, the Government of the Irish Free State, and the Government of Northern Ireland, and their respective peoples, make it desirable to amend and supplement the said Articles of Agreement, so as to avoid any causes of friction which might mar or retard the further growth of friendly relations between the said governments and peoples:

And whereas the British Government and the Government of the Irish Free State being united in amity in this undertaking with the Government of Northern Ireland, and being resolved mutually to aid one another in a spirit of neighbourly comradeship, hereby agree as follows:

1. The powers conferred by the proviso to Article 12 of the said Articles of Agreement on the Commission therein

mentioned are hereby revoked, and the extent of Northern Ireland for the purposes of the Government of Ireland Act, 1920, and of the said Articles of Agreement, shall be such as was fixed by subsection (2) of section one of that Act.

2. The Irish Free State is hereby released from the obligation under Article 5 of the said Articles of Agreement to assume the liability therein mentioned.

3. The Irish Free State hereby assumes all liability undertaken by the British Government in respect of malicious damage done since the twenty-first day of January nineteen hundred and nineteen to property in the area now under the jurisdiction of the Parliament and Government of the Irish Free State, and the Government of the Irish Free State shall repay the British Government, at such time or times and in such manner as may be agreed upon, moneys already paid by the British Government in respect of such damage, or liable to be so paid under obligations already incurred.

4. The Government of the Irish Free State hereby agrees to promote legislation increasing by ten per cent the measure of compensation under the Damage to Property (Compensation) Act, 1923, in respect of malicious damage to property done in the area now under the jurisdiction of the Parliament and Government of the Irish Free State between the eleventh day of July, nineteen hundred and twenty-one, and the twelfth day of May, nineteen hundred and twenty-three, and providing for the payment of such additional compensation by the issue of Five per cent Compensation Stock or Bonds.

5. The powers in relation to Northern Ireland which by the Government of Ireland Act, 1920, are made powers of the Council of Ireland, shall be and are hereby transferred to and shall become powers of the Parliament and the Government of Northern Ireland; and the Governments of the Irish Free State and of Northern Ireland shall meet together as and

when necessary for the purpose of considering matters of common interest arising out of or connected with the exercise and administration of the said powers.

6. This Agreement is subject to confirmation by the British Parliament and by the Oireachtas of the Irish Free State, and the Act of the British Parliament confirming this Agreement shall fix the date as from which the transfer of the powers of the Council of Ireland under this Agreement is to take effect.

Dated this 3rd day of December 1925.

Signed on behalf of the British Government.	*Signed on behalf of the Government of Irish Free State.*	*Signed on behalf of the Government of the Northern Ireland.*
Stanley Baldwin	Liam T. MacCosgair	James Craig
Winston S. Churchill	Kevin O'Higgins	Charles H. Blackmore.
W. Joynson-Hicks	Earnán de Blaghd	*Secretary to the Cabinet of Northern Ireland.*
Birkenhead		
L. S. Amery		

Appendix D

Extracts from the Irish Constitutions of 1922 and 1937

1 THE CONSTITUTION OF THE IRISH FREE STATE, 1922

Dáil Eireann sitting as a Constituent Assembly in this Provisional Parliament, acknowledging that all lawful authority comes from God to the people and in the confidence that the National life and unity of Ireland shall thus be restored, hereby proclaims the establishment of The Irish Free State (otherwise called Saorstát Eireann) and in the exercise of undoubted right, decrees and enacts as follows:-

1. The Constitution set forth in the First Schedule hereto annexed shall be the Constitution of The Irish Free State (Saorstát Eireann).

2. The said Constitution shall be construed with reference to the Articles of Agreement for a Treaty between Great Britain and Ireland set forth in the Second Schedule hereto annexed (hereinafter referred to as 'the Scheduled Treaty', which are hereby given the force of law, and if any provision of the said Constitution or of any amendment thereof or of any law made thereunder is in any respect repugnant to any of the provisions of the Scheduled Treaty, it shall, to the extent only of such repugnancy, be absolutely void and inoperative and the Parliament and the Executive Council of the Irish Free State (Saorstát Eireann) shall respectively pass such further legislation and do all such other things as may be necessary to implement the Scheduled Treaty.

3. This Act may be cited for all purposes as the Constitution of The Irish Free State (Saorstát Eireann) Act, 1922.

———————

———————

CONSTITUTION OF
THE IRISH FREE STATE
(SAORSTÁT EIREANN)

———————

Article 1
The Irish Free State (otherwise hereinafter called or sometimes called Saorstát Eireann) is a co-equal member of the Community of Nations forming the British Commonwealth of Nations.

Article 2
All powers of government and all authority legislative, executive, and judicial in Ireland, are derived from the people of Ireland, and the same shall be exercised in the Irish Free State (Saorstát Eireann) through the organisations established by or under, and in accord with, this Constitution.

Article 3
Every person, without distinction of sex, domiciled in the area of the jurisdiction of the Irish Free State (Saorstát Eireann) at the time of the coming into operation of this Constitution, who was born in Ireland or either of whose parents was born in Ireland or who has been ordinarily resident in the area of the jurisdiction of the Irish Free State (Saorstát Eireann) for not less than seven years, is a citizen of the Irish Free State (Saorstát Eireann) and shall within the limits of the jurisdiction of the Irish Free State (Saorstát Eireann) enjoy the privileges and be subject to the obligations of such citizenship: Provided that any such person being a citizen of another State may elect not to accept the citizenship hereby conferred; and the conditions governing the future acquisition and

termination of citizenship in the Irish Free State (Saorstát Eireann) shall be determined by law.

Article 4

The National language of the Irish Free State (Saorstát Eireann) is the Irish language, but the English language shall be equally recognised as an official language. Nothing in this Article shall prevent special provisions being made by the Parliament of the Irish Free State (otherwise called and herein generally referred to as the 'Oireachtas') for districts or areas in which only one language is in general use.

Article 5

No title of honour in respect of any services rendered in or in relation to the Irish Free State (Saorstát Eireann) may be conferred on any citizen of the Irish Free State (Saorstát Eireann) except with the approval or upon the advice of the Executive Council of the State.

Article 6

The liberty of the person is inviolable, and no person shall be deprived of his liberty except in accordance with law. Upon complaint made by or on behalf of any person that he is being unlawfully detained, the High Court and any and every judge thereof shall forthwith enquire into the same and may make an order requiring the person in whose custody such person shall be detained to produce the body of the person so detained before such Court or judge without delay and to certify in writing as to the cause of the detention and such Court or judge shall thereupon order the release of such person unless satisfied that he is being detained in accordance with the law:

Provided, however, that nothing in this Article contained shall be invoked to prohibit control or interfere with any act of the military forces of the Irish Free State (Saorstát Eireann) during the existence of a state of war or armed rebellion.

Article 7

The dwelling of each citizen is inviolable and shall not be forcibly entered except in accordance with law.

Article 8
Freedom of conscience and the free profession and practice of religion are, subject to public order and morality, guaranteed to every citizen, and no law may be made either directly or indirectly to endow any religion, or prohibit or restrict the free exercise thereof or give any preference, or impose any disability on account of religious belief or religious status, or affect prejudicially the right of any child to attend a school receiving public money without attending the religious instruction at the school, or make any discrimination as respects State aid between schools under the management of different religious denominations, or divert from any religious denomination or any educational institution any of its property except for the purpose of roads, railways, lighting, water or drainage works or other works of public utility, and on payment of compensation.

Article 9
The right of free expression of opinion as well as the right to assemble peaceably and without arms, and to form associations or unions is guaranteed for purposes not opposed to public morality. Laws regulating the manner in which the right of forming associations and the right of free assembly may be exercised shall contain no political, religious or class distinction.

Article 10
All citizens of the Irish Free State (Saorstát Eireann) have the right to free elementary education.

Article 11
All the lands and waters, mines and minerals, within the territory of the Irish Free State (Saorstát Eireann) hitherto vested in the State, or any department thereof, or held for the public use or benefit, and also all the natural resources of the same territory (including the air and all forms of potential energy), and also all royalties and franchises within that territory shall, from and after the date of the coming into

operation of this Constitution, belong to the Irish Free State (Saorstát Eireann), subject to any trusts, grants, leases or concessions then existing in respect thereof, or any valid private interest therein, and shall be controlled and administered by the Oireachtas, in accordance with such regulations and provisions as shall be from time to time approved by legislation, but the same shall not, nor shall any part thereof, be alienated, but may in the public interest be from time to time granted by way of lease or licence to be worked or enjoyed under the authority and subject to the control of the Oireachtas: Provided that no such lease or licence may be made for a term exceeding ninety-nine years, beginning from the date thereof, and no such lease or licence may be renewable by the terms thereof.

Article 12
A Legislature is hereby created to be known as the Oireachtas. It shall consist of the King and two Houses, the Chamber of Deputies (otherwise called and herein generally referred to as 'Dáil Eireann') and the Senate (otherwise called and herein generally referred to as 'Seanad Eireann'). The sole and exclusive power of making laws for the peace, order and good government of the Irish Free State (Saorstát Eireann) is vested in the Oireachtas.

Article 13
The Oireachtas shall sit in or near the city of Dublin or in such other place as from time to time it may determine.

Article 14
All citizens of the Irish Free State (Saorstát Eireann) without distinction of sex, who have reached the age of twenty-one years and who comply with the provisions of the prevailing electoral laws, shall have the right to vote for members of Dáil Eireann, and to take part in the Referendum and Initiative. All citizens of the Irish Free State (Saorstát Eireann) without distinction of sex who have reached the age of thirty years and who comply with the provisions of the prevailing electoral

laws, shall have the right to vote for members of Seanad Eireann. No voter may exercise more than one vote at an election to either House and the voting shall be by secret ballot. The mode and place of exercising this right shall be determined by law.

Article 15
Every citizen who has reached the age of twenty-one years and who is not placed under disability or incapacity by the Constitution or by law shall be eligible to become a member of Dáil Eireann.

Article 16
No person may be at the same time a member both of Dáil Eireann and of Seanad Eireann, and if any person who is already a member of either House is elected to be a member of the other House, he shall forthwith be deemed to have vacated his first seat.

Article 17
The oath to be taken by members of the Oireachtas shall be in the following form:-

I _____ do solemnly swear true faith and allegiance to the Constitution of the Irish Free State as by law established, and that I will be faithful to H.M. King George V., his heirs and successors by law in virtue of the common citizenship of Ireland with Great Britain and her adherence to and membership of the group of nations forming the British Commonwealth of Nations.

Such oath shall be taken and subscribed by every member of the Oireachtas before taking his seat therein before the Representative of the Crown or some person authorised by him.

[The Constitution contains further Articles: 18–83]

2   BUNREACHT NA HÉIREANN, 1937

In the Name of the Most Holy Trinity, from Whom is all authority and to Whom, as our final end, all actions both of men and States must be referred,

We, the people of Éire,

Humbly acknowledging all our obligations to our Divine Lord, Jesus Christ, Who sustained our fathers through centuries of trial

Gratefully remembering their heroic and unremitting struggle to regain the rightful independence of our Nation,

And seeking to promote the common good, with due observance of Prudence, Justice and Charity, so that the dignity and freedom of the individual may be assured, true social order attained, the unity of our country restored, and concord established with other nations,

Do hereby adopt, enact, and give to ourselves this Constitution.

THE NATION

Article 1
The Irish nation hereby affirms its inalienable, indefeasible and sovereign right to choose its own form of Government, to determine its relations with other nations, and to develop its life, political, economic and cultural, in accordance with its own genius and traditions.

Article 2
The national territory consist of the whole island of Ireland, its islands and the territorial seas.

Article 3
Pending the re-integration of the national territory, and without prejudice to the right of the Parliament and Government

established by this Constitution to exercise jurisdiction over the whole of that territory, the laws enacted by that Parliament shall have the like area and extent of application as the laws of Saorstát Éireann and the like extra-territorial effect.

THE STATE

Article 4
The name of the state is Éire, or in the English language, *Ireland*.

Article 5
Ireland is a sovereign, independent, democratic state.

Article 6
1.   All powers of government, legislative, executive and judicial, derive, under God, from the people, whose right it is to designate the rulers of the State and, in final appeal, to decide all questions of national policy, according to the requirements of the common good.

2.   These powers of government are exercisable only by or on the authority of the organs of State established by this Constitution.

Article 7
The national flag is the tricolour of green, white and orange.

Article 8
1.   The Irish language as the national language is the first official language.

2.   The English language is recognised as a second official language.

3.   Provision may, however, be made by law for the exclusive use of either of the said languages for any one or more official purposes, either throughout the State or in any part thereof.

Article 9

1. (1) On the coming into operation of this Constitution any person who was a citizen of Saorstát Éireann immediately before the coming into operation of this Constitution shall become and be a citizen of Ireland.

(2) The future acquisition and loss of Irish nationality and citizenship shall be determined in accordance with law.

(3) No person may be excluded from Irish nationality and citizenship by reason of the sex of such person.

2. Fidelity to the nation and loyalty to the State are fundamental political duties of all citizens.

Article 10

1. All natural resources, including the air and all forms of potential energy, within the jurisdiction of the Parliament and Government established by this Constitution and all royalties and franchises within that jurisdiction belong to the State subject to all estates and interests therein for the time being lawfully vested in any person or body.

2. All land and all mines, minerals and waters which belonged to Saorstát Éireann immediately before the coming into operation of this Constitution belong to the State to the same extent as they then belonged to Saorstát Éireann.

THE FAMILY

Article 41

1. (1) The State recognises the Family as the natural primary and fundamental unit group of Society, and as a moral institution possessing inalienable and imprescriptible rights, antecedent and superior to all positive law.

(2) The State, therefore, guarantees to protect the Family in its constitution and authority, as the necessary basis of social order and as indispensable to the welfare of the Nation and the State.

2. (1) In particular, the State recognises that by her life within the home, woman gives to the State a support without which the common good cannot be achieved.

    (2) The State shall, therefore, endeavour to ensure that mothers shall not be obliged by economic necessity to engage in labour to the neglect of their duties in the home.

3. (1) The State pledges itself to guard with special care the institution of Marriage, on which the Family is founded, and to protect it against attack.

    (2) No law shall be enacted providing for the grant of a dissolution of marriage.

    (3) No person whose marriage has been dissolved under the civil law of any other State but is a subsisting valid marriage under the law for the time being in force within the jurisdiction of the Government and Parliament established by this Constitution shall be capable of contracting a valid marriage within that jurisdiction during the lifetime of the other party to the marriage so dissolved.

RELIGION

Article 44

1. (1) The State acknowledges that the homage of public worship is due to Almighty God. It shall hold His Name in reverence, and shall respect and honour religion.

    (2) The State recognises the special position of the Holy Catholic Apostolic and Roman Church as the guardian of the Faith professed by the great majority of the citizens.

    (3) The State also recognises the Church of Ireland, the Presbyterian Church in Ireland, the Methodist Church in Ireland, the Religious Society of Friends in Ireland, as well as the Jewish Congregations and the other religious denominations existing in Ireland at the date of the coming into operation of this Constitution.

2. (1) Freedom of conscience and the free profession and practice of religion are, subject to public order and morality, guaranteed to every citizen.

    (2) The State guarantees not to endow any religion.

    (3) The State shall not impose any disabilities or make any discrimination on the ground of religious profession, belief or status.

    (4) Legislation providing State aid for schools shall not discriminate between schools under the management of different religious denominations, nor be such as to affect prejudicially the right of any child to attend a school receiving public money without attending religious instruction at that school.

    (5) Every religious denomination shall have the right to manage its own affairs, own, acquire and administer property, movable and immovable, and maintain institutions for religious or charitable purposes.

    (6) The property of any religious denomination or any educational institution shall not be diverted save for necessary works of public utility and on payment of compensation.

[The 1937 Constitution contains, in total, 50 Articles.]

Appendix E(1)

The Republic of Ireland Act, 1948

AN ACT TO REPEAL THE EXECUTIVE AUTHORITY (EXTERNAL RELATIONS) ACT, 1936, TO DECLARE THAT THE DESCRIPTION OF THE STATE SHALL BE THE REPUBLIC OF IRELAND, AND TO ENABLE THE PRESIDENT TO EXERCISE THE EXECUTIVE POWER OR ANY EXECUTIVE FUNCTION OF THE STATE IN OR IN CONNECTION WITH ITS EXTERNAL RELATIONS.   [*21st December 1948.*]

Be it enacted by the Oireachtas as follows:

Repeal of the Executive Authority (External Relations) Act, 1936.

1.   The Executive Authority (External Relations) Act, 1936 (No. 58 of 1936), is hereby repealed.

The Republic of Ireland

2.   It is hereby declared that the description of the State shall be the Republic of Ireland.

Exercise by the President of the executive power or any executive function of the State in or in connection with its external relations.

3.   The President, on the authority and on the advice of the Government, may exercise the executive power or any executive function of the State in or in connection with its external relations.

Commencement.

4.   This Act shall come into operation on such day as the Government may by order appoint.

Short title.

5.   This Act may be cited as The Republic of Ireland Act, 1948.

Appendix E(2)

The Ireland Act, 1949

An Act to recognise and declare the constitutional position as to the part of Ireland heretofore known as Eire, and to make provision as to the name by which it may be known and the manner in which the law is to apply in relation to it; to declare and affirm the constitutional position and the territorial integrity of Northern Ireland and to amend, as respects the parliament of the United Kingdom, the law relating to the qualifications of electors in constituencies in Northern Ireland; and for purposes connected with the matters aforesaid. (*2nd June 1949*)

Be it enacted by the King's most Excellent Majesty, by and with the advice and consent of the Lords Spiritual and Temporal, and Commons, in this present Parliament assembled, and by the authority of the same, as follows:-

1. (1) It is hereby recognized and declared that the part of Ireland heretofore known as Eire ceased, as from the eighteenth day of April, nineteen hundred and forty-nine, to be part of His Majesty's dominions.

(2) It is hereby declared that Northern Ireland remains part of His Majesty's dominions and of the United Kingdom and it is hereby affirmed that in no event will Northern Ireland or any part thereof cease to be part of His Majesty's dominions and of the United Kingdom without the consent of the Parliament of Northern Ireland.

(3) The part of Ireland referred to in subsection (1) of this section is hereafter in this Act referred to, and may in any Act, enactment or instrument passed or made after the passing of this Act be referred to, by the name attributed thereto by the law thereof, that is to say, as the Republic of Ireland.

2. (1) It is hereby declared that, notwithstanding that the Republic of Ireland is not part of His Majesty's dominions, the Republic of Ireland is not a foreign country for the purposes of any law in force in any part of the United Kingdom or in any colony, protectorate or United Kingdom trust territory, whether by virtue of a rule of law or of an Act of Parliament or any other enactment or instrument whatsoever, whether passed or made before or after the passing of this Act, and references in any Act of Parliament, other enactment or instrument whatsoever, whether passed or made before or after the passing of this Act, to foreigners, aliens, foreign countries, and foreign or foreign-built ships or aircraft shall be construed accordingly.

(2) The person who, in the United Kingdom, is the chief representative of the Republic of Ireland or of the Government thereof shall, whatever the style of his office, have the same privileges and exemptions as to taxation and otherwise as fall to be accorded under the law for the time being in force to High Commissioners and Agents General within the meaning of section nineteen of the Finance Act, 1923, and his staff shall have the same privileges and exemptions as to taxation and otherwise as fall to be accorded under the law for the time being in force to their staffs.

3. (1) It is hereby declared that —
(a) the operation of the following statutory provisions, that is to say —
(i) the British Nationality Act, 1948 (and in particular, and without prejudice to the generality of the preceding words, sections two, three and six thereof);
(ii) so much of any Act, or of any Act of the Parliament of Northern Ireland, as gives effect, or enables effect to be given, to agreements or arrangements made at any time after the coming into operation of the original constitution of the Irish Free State, being agreements or arrangements made with the Government of, or otherwise affecting, the part of Ireland which now forms the

Republic of Ireland, including agreements or arrangements made after the commencement of this Act; and
(iii) the Orders in Council made under sections five and six of the Irish Free State (Consequential Provisions) Act, 1922 (Session 2), is not affected by the fact that the Republic of Ireland is not part of His Majesty's dominions; and

(b) that, in the said provisions, and in any Act of Parliament or other enactment or instrument whatsoever, so far as it operates as part of the law of, or of any part of, the United Kingdom or any colony, protectorate or United Kingdom trust territory, references to citizens of Eire include, on their true construction, references to citizens of the Republic of Ireland.

(2)   Until provision to the contrary is made by Parliament or by some other authority having power in that behalf, the following provisions shall have effect as respects any Act of Parliament or other enactment or instrument whatsoever passed or made before the passing of this Act, so far as it operates as part of the law of, or of any part of, the United Kingdom or any colony, protectorate or United Kingdom trust territory, that is to say —

(a) if it contains a reference to His Majesty's dominions, or to any parts thereof, which would have extended so as in any way to include the Republic of Ireland had that part of Ireland remained part of His Majesty's dominions, it shall have effect, with any necessary adaptations, as if that reference did extend so as in that way to include the Republic of Ireland, notwithstanding that that part of Ireland is no longer part of His Majesty's dominions; and

(b) in particular and without prejudice to the generality of the preceding paragraph, if it contains a reference to all, or to any classes or descriptions of, British or British-built ships or aircraft which would have extended so as in any way to include all, or any classes or descriptions of, the ships or aircraft of or built in the Republic of Ireland had that part of Ireland remained part of His Majesty's dominions, it shall have effect, with any necessary adaptations, as if that reference did extend so as in that way to include all, or that class or description of, the ships or aircraft of or built in the Republic of Ireland, as the case may be, notwithstanding that that part of Ireland is no longer part of His Majesty's dominions.

(3) The last preceding subsection shall not apply to so much of section two of the Regency Act, 1937, as requires that a declaration under that section of the incapacity or unavailability of the Sovereign should be communicated to the Governments of His Majesty's dominions, and nothing in this section shall be construed as implying that any alteration in the law touching the Succession to the Throne or the Royal Style and Titles requires the assent of the Parliament of the Republic of Ireland.

4. (1) Subject to the provisions of subsection (4) of this section, subsection (2) of section three of the British Nationality Act, 1948 (which relates to the effect of existing Acts of Parliament and other enactments and instruments) shall have effect in relation to Acts, enactments or instruments passed or made before the end of the year nineteen hundred and forty-nine as it has effect in relation to Acts, enactments or instruments in force at the date of the commencement of that Act.

(2) Subject to the provisions of subsection (4) of this section, subsection (2) of the last preceding section shall have effect in relation to Acts, enactments or instruments passed or made before the end of the year nineteen hundred and forty-nine as it has effect in relation to Acts, enactments or instruments passed or made before the passing of this Act.

(3) Where, whether by virtue of the preceding provisions of this section or otherwise, subsection (2) of the section three of the British Nationality Act, 1948, or subsection (2) of the last preceding section has effect in relation to any Act, enactment

or instrument, it shall, subject to the provisions of subsection (4) of this section, have effect also in relation to any other Act, enactment or instrument which, whether expressly or by implication, is required to be construed in the same way as that Act, enactment or instrument.

(4) The preceding provisions of this section have effect in relation to any Act, enactment or instrument only in so far as a contrary intention does not appear in that Act, enactment or instrument:

Provided that the fact that an Act, enactment or instrument refers to a British subject, or to, or to any part of, His Majesty's dominions, or to a British or British-built ship or aircraft, without referring to a citizen of the Republic of Ireland, to the Republic of Ireland or to a ship or aircraft of or built in the Republic of Ireland shall not of itself be taken as indicating a contrary intention for the purposes of this subsection, and the same principle of construction shall applied to other similar expressions.

5. (1) A person who (a) was born before the sixth day of December, nineteen hundred and twenty-two, in the part of Ireland which now forms the Republic of Ireland; and (b) was a British subject immediately before the date of commencement of the British Nationality Act, 1948,

shall not be deemed to have ceased to be a British subject on the coming into force of that Act unless either —

(i) he was, on the said sixth day of December, domiciled in the part of Ireland which now forms the Republic of Ireland; or (ii) he was, on or after the tenth day of April nineteen hundred and thirty-five and before the date of the commencement of that Act, permanently resident in that part of Ireland; or (iii) he had, before the date of the commencement of that Act, been registered as a citizen of Eire under the laws of that part of Ireland relating to citizenship.

(2) In relation to persons born before the said sixth day of December in the part of Ireland which now forms the

Republic of Ireland, being persons who do not satisfy any of the conditions specified in paragraphs (i), (ii), and (iii) of subsection (1) of this sections twelve and thirteen of the said Act (which relate to citizenship of the United Kingdom and Colonies and to British subjects without citizenship) shall have effect and be deemed always to have effect as if, in paragraph (a) of subsection (4) of the said section twelve, the words 'or a citizen of Eire' and in subsection (1) of the said section thirteen, the words 'or of Eire' were omitted.

(3) So much of the said Act as has the effect of providing that a person is, in specified circumstances, to be treated for the purposes of that Act as having been a British subject immediately before the commencement thereof shall apply also for the purposes of this section.

(4) Nothing in this section affects the position of any person who, on the coming into force of the British Nationality Act, 1948, became a citizen of the United Kingdom and Colonies or a British subject without citizenship apart from the provisions of this section.

6. (1) Notwithstanding anything in the Representation of the People Act, 1948, a person shall not be entitled to vote as an elector of an election of a person to serve as a Member of the Parliament of the United Kingdom for a constituency in Northern Ireland unless he was resident in Northern Ireland during the whole of the period of three months ending on the qualifying date for that election.

(2) Subsection (2) of section two of the Representation of the People Act, 1948 (which specifies the cases where a person's residence is not to be deemed to be interrupted) and subsection (3) of that section (which provides that a person detained in a mental hospital or prison is not to be treated as resident there) shall apply for the purposes of the preceding subsection as they apply for the purposes of section one of that Act.

(3) The preceding provisions of this section shall not affect the right to vote of any service voter, and a person ceasing to have a service qualification shall be treated for the purposes of subsection (1) of this section as if he were resident

in Northern Ireland during the period during which he had a service qualification.

(4) The register of parliamentary electors shall, for the purposes of Part 1 of the Representation of the People Act, 1948, be conclusive on the question whether or not a person registered as an elector in a constituency in Northern Ireland was resident in Northern Ireland during the whole of the period of three months ending on the qualifying date.

(5) This section shall be construed as if enacted in Part 1 of the Representation of the People Act, 1948:

Provided that this section shall not have effect with respect to the first register to be prepared under that Act or the elections, if any, for which that register is used.

7. (1) This Act may be cited as the Ireland Act, 1949.

(2) References in this Act to colonies, protectorates and United Kingdom trust territories shall be construed as if they were references contained in the British Nationality Act, 1948.

(3) Save as otherwise expressly provided, this Act shall be deemed to have had effect as from the eighteenth day of April, nineteen hundred and forty-nine.

Acts. Parl UK, 1949 (12 and 13 Geo. VI, cap. 41)

APPENDIX F

THE ANGLO-IRISH AGREEMENT, 15 NOVEMBER 1985

AGREEMENT
between
THE GOVERNMENT OF IRELAND
and
THE GOVERNMENT OF THE UNITED KINGDOM

The Government of Ireland and the Government of the United Kingdom:

Wishing further to develop the unique relationship between their peoples and the close co-operation between their countries as friendly neighbours and as partners in the European Community;

Recognising the major interest of both their countries and, above all, of the people of Northern Ireland in diminishing the divisions there and achieving lasting peace and stability;

Recognising the need for continuing efforts to reconcile and to acknowledge the rights of the two major traditions that exist in Ireland, represented on the one hand by those who wish for no change in the present status of Northern Ireland and on the other hand by those who aspire to a sovereign united Ireland achieved by peaceful means and through agreement;

Reaffirming their total rejection of any attempt to promote political objectives by violence or the threat of violence and their determination to work together to ensure that those who adopt or support such methods do not succeed;

Recognising that a condition of genuine reconciliation and dialogue between unionists and nationalists is mutual recognition and acceptance of each other's rights;

Recognising and respecting the identities of the two communities in Northern Ireland, and the right of each to pursue its aspirations by peaceful and constitutional means;

Reaffirming their commitment to a society in Northern Ireland in which all may live in peace, free from discrimination and intolerance, and with the opportunity for both communities to participate fully in the structures and processes of government;

Have accordingly agreed as follows:

A
STATUS OF NORTHERN IRELAND

ARTICLE 1

The two Governments

(a) affirm that any change in the status of Northern Ireland would only come about with the consent of a majority of the people of Northern Ireland;

(b) recognise that the present wish of a majority of the people of Northern Ireland is for no change in the status of Northern Ireland;

(c) declare that, if in the future a majority of the people of Northern Ireland clearly wish for and formally consent to the establishment of a united Ireland, they will introduce and support in the respective Parliaments legislation to give effect to that wish.

B
THE INTERGOVERNMENTAL CONFERENCE

ARTICLE 2

(a) There is hereby established, within the framework of the Anglo-Irish Intergovernmental Council set up after the meeting between the two Heads of Government on

6 November 1981, an Intergovernmental Conference (hereinafter referred to as 'the Conference'), concerned with Northern Ireland and with relations between the two parts of the island of Ireland, to deal, as set out in this Agreement, on a regular basis with

   (i)   political matters;
  (ii)   security and related matters;
 (iii)   legal matters, including the administration of justice;
 (iv)   the promotion of cross-Border co-operation.

(b) The United Kingdom Government accept that the Irish Government will put forward views and proposals on matters relating to Northern Ireland within the field of activity of the Conference in so far as those matters are not the responsibility of a devolved administration in Northern Ireland. In the interest of promoting peace and stability, determined efforts shall be made through the Conference to resolve any differences. The Conference will be mainly concerned with Northern Ireland; but some of the matters under consideration will involve co-operative action in both parts of the island of Ireland, and possibly also in Great Britain. Some of the proposals considered in respect of Northern Ireland may also be found to have application by the Irish Government. There is no derogation from the sovereignty of either the Irish Government or the United Kingdom Government, and each retains responsibility for the decisions and administration of government within its own jurisdiction.

ARTICLE 3

The Conference shall meet at ministerial or official level, as required. The business of the Conference will thus receive attention at the highest level. Regular and frequent ministerial meetings shall be held; and in particular special meetings shall be convened at the request of either side. Officials may meet in subordinate groups. Membership of the Conference and of sub-groups shall be small and flexible. When the Conference meets at ministerial level an Irish Minister designated as the Permanent Irish Ministerial Representative and the Secretary of State for Northern Ireland shall be joint chairmen. Within the framework of the Conference other Irish and British Ministers may hold or attend meetings as appropriate: when legal matters are under consideration the Attorneys General may attend. Ministers may be accompanied by their officials and their professional advisers: for example, when questions of security policy or security co-operation are being discussed, they may be accompanied by the Commissioner of the Garda Síochána and the Chief Constable of the Royal Ulster Constabulary; or when questions of economic or social policy or co-operation are being discussed, they may be accompanied by officials of the relevant Departments. A Secretariat shall be established by the two Governments to service the Conference on a continuing basis in the discharge of its function as set out in this agreement.

ARTICLE 4

(a)   In relation to matters coming within its field of activity, the Conference shall be a framework within which the Irish Government and the United Kingdom Government work together

    (i)   for the accommodation of the rights and identities of the two traditions which exist in Northern Ireland; and (ii) for peace, stability and prosperity throughout the island of Ireland by promoting reconciliation, respect for human rights, co-operation against terrorism and the development of economic, social and cultural co-operation.

(b)   It is the declared policy of the United Kingdom Government that responsibility in respect of certain matters within the powers of the Secretary of State for Northern Ireland should be devolved within Northern

Ireland on a basis which would secure widespread acceptance throughout the community. The Irish Government support that policy.

(c) Both Governments recognise that devolution can be achieved only with the co-operation of constitutional representatives within Northern Ireland of both traditions there. The Conference shall be a framework within which the Irish Government may put forward views and proposals on the modalities of bringing about devolution in Northern Ireland, in so far as they relate to the interests of the minority community.

C
POLITICAL MATTERS

ARTICLE 5

(a) The Conference shall concern itself with measures to recognise and accommodate the rights and identities of the two traditions in Northern Ireland, to protect human rights and to prevent discrimination. Matters to be considered in this area include measures to foster the cultural heritage of both traditions, changes in electoral arrangements, the use of flags and emblems, the avoidance of economic and social discrimination and the advantages and disadvantages of a Bill of Rights in some form in Northern Ireland.

(b) The discussion of these matters shall be mainly concerned with Northern Ireland, but the possible application of any measures pursuant to this Article by the Irish Government in their jurisdiction shall not be excluded.

(c) If it should prove impossible to achieve and sustain devolution on a basis which secures widespread acceptance in Northern Ireland, the Conference shall be a framework within which the Irish Government may, where the interests of the minority community are significantly or especially affected, put forward views on proposals for major legislation and on major policy issues, which are within the purview of the Northern Ireland Departments and which remain the responsibility of the Secretary of State for Northern Ireland.

ARTICLE 6

The Conference shall be a framework within which the Irish Government may put forward views and proposals on the role and composition of bodies appointed by the Secretary of State for Northern Ireland or by Departments subject to his direction and control including

the Standing Advisory Commission on Human Rights;
the Fair Employment Agency;
the Equal Opportunities Commission;
the Police Authority for Northern Ireland;
the Police Complaints Board.

D
SECURITY AND RELATED MATTERS

ARTICLE 7

(a)   The Conference shall consider
 (i)   security policy;
(ii)   relations between the security forces and the community;
(iii)   prisons policy.

(b)   The Conference shall consider the security situation at its regular meetings and thus provide an opportunity to address policy issues, serious incidents and forthcoming events.

(c)   The two Governments agree that there is a need for a programme of special measures in Northern Ireland to improve relations between the security forces and the community with the object in particular of making the security forces more readily accepted by the nationalist community. Such a programme shall be developed, for the Conference's consideration, and may include the establishment of local consultative machinery, training in community relations, crime prevention schemes involving the community, improvements in arrangements for handling complaints, and action to increase the proportion of members of the minority in the Royal Ulster Constabulary. Elements of the programme may be considered by the Irish Government suitable for application within their jurisdiction.

(d)   The Conference may consider policy issues relating to prisons. Individual cases may be raised as appropriate, so that information can be provided or inquiries instituted.

E
LEGAL MATTERS, INCLUDING
THE ADMINISTRATION OF JUSTICE

ARTICLE 8

The Conference shall deal with issues of concern to both countries relating to the enforcement of the criminal law. In particular it shall consider whether there are areas of the criminal law applying in the North and in the South respectively which might with benefit be harmonised. The two Governments agree on the importance of public confidence in the administration of justice. The conference shall seek, with the help of advice from experts as appropriate, measures which would give substantial expression to this aim, considering inter alia the possibility of mixed courts in both jurisdictions for the trial of certain offences. The Conference shall also be concerned with policy aspects of extradition and extra-territorial jurisdiction as between North and South.

F
CROSS-BORDER CO-OPERATION ON SECURITY, ECONOMIC, SOCIAL AND CULTURAL MATTERS

ARTICLE 9

(a) With a view to enhancing cross-Border co-operation on security matters, the Conference shall set in hand a programme of work to be undertaken by the Commissioner of the Garda Síochána and the Chief Constable of the Royal Ulster Constabulary and, where appropriate, groups of officials, in such areas as threat assessments, exchange of information, liaison structures, technical co-operation, training of personnel, and operational resources.

(b) The Conference shall have no operational responsibilities; responsibility for police operations shall remain with the heads of the respective police forces, the Commissioner of the Garda Síochána maintaining his links with the Minister for Justice and the Chief Constable of the Royal Ulster Constabulary his links with the Secretary of State for Northern Ireland.

ARTICLE 10

(a) The two Governments shall co-operate to promote the economic and social development of those areas of both parts of Ireland which have suffered most severely from the consequences of the instability of recent years, and shall consider the possibility of securing international support for this work.

(b)   If it should prove impossible to achieve and sustain devolution on a basis which secures widespread acceptance in Northern Ireland, the Conference shall be a framework for the promotion of co-operation between the two parts of Ireland concerning cross-Border aspects of economic, social and cultural matters in relation to which the Secretary of State for Northern Ireland continues to exercise authority.

(c)   If responsibility is devolved in respect of certain matters in the economic, social or cultural areas currently within the responsibility of the Secretary of State for Northern Ireland, machinery will need to be established by the responsible authorities in the North and South for practical co-operation in respect of cross-Border aspects of these issues.

G
ARRANGEMENTS FOR REVIEW

ARTICLE 11

At the end of three years from signature of this Agreement, or earlier if requested by either Government, the working of the Conference shall be reviewed by the two Governments to see whether any changes in the scope and nature of its activities are desirable.

H
INTERPARLIAMENTARY RELATIONS

ARTICLE 12

It will be for Parliamentary decision in Dublin and in Westminster whether to establish an Anglo-Irish Parliamentary body of the kind adumbrated in the Anglo-Irish Studies

Report of November 1981. The two Governments agree that they would give support as appropriate to such a body, if it were to be established.

I
FINAL CLAUSES

ARTICLE 13

This Agreement shall enter into force on the date on which the two Governments exchange notifications of their acceptance of this Agreement.

In witness whereof the undersigned, being duly authorised thereto by their respective Governments, have signed this Agreement.

Done in two originals at Hillsborough
on the 15th day of November 1985

For the Government of Ireland,
Gearóid Mac Gearailt

For the Government of the United Kingdom,
Margaret Thatcher.

NOTES

NOTES TO CHAPTER 1

1. *The Repealer Repulsed! A Correct Narrative of the Rise and Progress of the Repeal Invasion of Ulster: Dr Cooke's Challenge and Mr O'Connell's Tactics and Flight, etc.*, published by William M'Comb (Belfast, 1841), p. 111.
2. D. Gwynn, *The Life of John Redmond* (London, 1932), p. 232.
3. J. A. Spender, *Life of Sir Henry Campbell-Bannerman* (London, 1923), vol. II, p. 339.
4. F. S. L. Lyons, *Ireland since the Famine* (London, 1971), p. 262.
5. Ibid., p. 264.
6. See 'Select Documents XXXII: the IRB Supreme Council, 1868–78', presented by T. W. Moody and Leon O'Broin in *Irish Historical Studies*, vol. XIX, no. 75 (March 1975), pp. 299–313. Quotations are from pp. 199–302, 309 and 313.
7. C. Gavan Duffy, *Thomas Davis: A Memoir* (London, 1895), p. 66.
8. Thomas Davis, 'An Address Read before the Historical Society, Dublin, 16 June 1840', quoted in Robert Kee, *The Green Flag*, vol. 1: *The Most Distressful Country* (London, 1976), p. 196.
9. John Redmond, *House of Commons Debates* (hereafter *HC Debs*), vol. XXXIX, cols 1085-6 (13 June 1912).
10. H. H. Asquith, *HC Debs*, vol. XXXVI, col. 1407 (12 April 1912).
11. Redmond, ibid., cols 1086–7.
12. Ibid., col. 1086. Redmond is here quoting *The New Irish Constitution: Exposition and Arguments*, ed. J. H. Morgan (London, 1912) published that week.
13. Ibid., col. 1088.
14. Ibid.
15. Ibid. vol. XLVI, col. 405 (1 January 1913).

16. *Ulster's Solemn League and Covenant.* See, for this copy, Patrick Buckland, *Irish Unionism 1885–1923: a Documentary History* (Belfast, 1973), p. 224.
17. Ronald McNeill, *Ulster's Stand for Union* (New York, 1920), p. 107.
18. Lord Salisbury at the Ulster Hall, 27 September 1912. See *Belfast Newsletter*, 28 September 1912.
19. See R. J. Lawrence, *The Government of Northern Ireland* (Oxford, 1965), p. 13, quoting from S. Rosenbaum (ed.), *Against Home Rule* (London, 1912), p. 18

NOTES TO CHAPTER 2

1. Sir Edward Carson, *HC Debs*, vol. LIX, col. 934 (9 March 1914).
2. *Suspensory Act, 1914* (4 and 5 Geo V, cap 88).
3. H. H. Asquith, *H. C. Debs*, vol. LXVI, cols 891–2 (15 Sept. 1914).
4. John Redmond, *H. C. Debs*, vol. LXV, col. 1829 (3 August 1914). For 20 September see S. Gwynne, *John Redmond's Last Years* (London, 1919), p. 155.
5. Terence Denman, *Ireland's Unknown Soldiers* (Dublin, 1992), p. 29 (quoting Redmond's *A Visit to the Front* (London, 1915), p. 38).
6. Ibid., p. 21.
7. Ibid., p. 37.
8. Traditional ballad.
9. *Proclamation of the Republic.* See, for example, A. Mitchell and P. O'Snodaigh, *Irish Political Documents 1916–1949* (Dublin, 1985), pp. 17–18.
10. R. F. Foster, *Modern Ireland 1600–1972* (London, 1988), p. 479.
11. See D. W. Harkness, 'Unknown Master of a Bitter Lesson', in *Irish Press*, 10 November 1979, *Pearse Supplement*, p. VII.
12. Adam Duffin, in P. Buckland, *Irish Unionism 1885–1923: a Documentary History* (Belfast, 1973), p. 404.
13. R. McNeill, *Ulster's Stand for Union* (New York,1920), p. 244.
14. A. T. Q. Stewart, *Edward Carson* (Dublin, 1981), p. 103.
15. Buckland, *Irish Unionism*, pp. 404–5.
16. Lord Lansdowne, *House of Lords Debates* (hereafter *HL Debs*), vol. XXII, col. 646 (11 July 1916).
17. F. S. L. Lyons, *Ireland since the Famine* (London, 1971), p. 389. See also Michael Laffan, 'The Unification of Sinn Fein', in *Irish Historical Studies*, vol. XVII, no. 67 (March, 1971), pp. 353–79.

18.	M. Laffan, *The Partition of Ireland, 1911–1925* (Dundalk, 1983), p. 57.

NOTES TO CHAPTER 3

1.	See W. S. Churchill's disdainful comment in the House of Commons, 16 February 1922: *HC Debs*, vol. 150, col. 1270.
2.	10 and 11 Geo V, cap. 67 (23 December 1920) Government of Ireland Act, 1920, Article 75 and Article 1 (2).
3.	Letter from Sir J. Stronge to H. de F. Montgomery, 12 March 1923, Public Record Office, Northern Ireland (hereafter PRONI), D627/435, cited in P. Buckland, *Irish Unionism 1885–1923: a Documentary History* (Belfast,1973), p. 417.
4.	See *Ulster and Home Rule: No Partition of Ulster,* a pamphlet issued by delegates from Cavan, Donegal and Monaghan, in April 1920, quoted in Buckland, *Irish Unionism,* pp. 412–16.
5.	J. J. Lee, *Ireland 1912–1985* (Cambridge, 1989), p. 45.
6.	Craig to Lloyd George, 11 November 1921, in *Correspondence between HMG and the Prime Minister of Northern Ireland etc.,* Cmnd 1561 (1921) p. 5
7.	*Northern Ireland House of Commons Debates* (hereafter *NIHC Debs*) (20 September 1921), vol. 1, col. 61.
8.	Lloyd George to de Valera, 19 September 1921, in *Dail Eireann, Official Correspondence relating to the Peace Negotiations, June–September 1921* (Dublin, October 1921), pp. 22–3.
9.	See David Harkness,'The Ill-fated Boundary Commission and a Rebuke for Craig', in *Irish Times, Supplement,* 21 April 1976, p. 6.
10.	*Articles of Agreement for a Treaty between Great Britain and Ireland* (signed in London on 6 December 1921), Article 12.
11.	*NIHC Debs* (20 September 1921), vol. 1, col. 49, Craig, quoting his letter of 29 July 1921 to Lloyd George.
12.	David Harkness, 'Ill-fated Boundary Commission'.
13.	Ibid.
14.	*HL Debs* (12 March 1922), vol. 49, col. 757.
15.	Geoffrey Hand (ed.), *Report of the Irish Boundary Commission, 1925* (Shannon, 1989), p. 29.
16.	15 and 16 Geo V, cap. 77, 'Agreement amending and supplementing the Articles of Agreement for a Treaty between Great Britain and Ireland, December 3, 1925'. This is also Irish Free State Act No. 40 of 1925.

Notes

NOTES TO CHAPTER 4

1. J. M. Andrews, PRONI CAB 4/172/23 (29 June 1926).
2. For a discussion of these issues see Clare O'Halloran, *Partition and the Limits of Irish Nationalism* (Dublin, 1987), ch 4.
3. Craig to Sir James O'Grady, PRONI CAB 9B/201/1.
4. Londonderry to Craig, ibid.
5. Public Record Office, London (hereafter PRO), CAB 24, 262, CP 124(36), App. 1, p. 2. See also David Harkness, 'Mr de Valera's Dominion: Irish Relations with Britain and the Commonwealth, 1932–1938', in *Journal of Commonwealth Political Studies*, vol. VIII, no. 3 (1970), pp. 206–28.
6. PRO CAB 27, 525,ISC (32), 7.
7. *Northern Whig*, 12 April 1932.
8. PRONI CAB 9F/57/1.
9. PRONI FIN 30/L/2.
10. Dennis Kennedy, *The Widening Gulf: Northern Attitudes to the Independent Irish State, 1919–49* (Belfast, 1988), p. 167.
11. NIHC Debs, vol. xvi, col. 1095 (24 April 1934).
12. Kennedy, *Widening Gulf*, ch. 11.
13. *Belfast Newsletter*, 29 November 1933.
14. *Irish Independent*, 15, 17, 22 and 24 July 1935.
15. See Harkness, 'Mr de Valera's Dominion', p. 220.
16. *Belfast Newsletter*, 12 and 14 December 1936.
17. *Bunreacht na hEireann* (The Irish Constitution) Dublin, 1937).
18. *Belfast Newsletter*, 1 May 1937.
19. Ibid., 14 May 1937.
20. J. J. Lee and Gearoid O'Tuathaigh, *The Age of de Valera* (Dublin, 1982), pp. 104–5, and 99.
21. Maurice Moynihan (ed.), *Speeches and Statements by Eamon de Valera, 1917–73* (Dublin, 1980), p. 330 (12 October 1937).
22. D. S. Johnson, 'Northern Ireland as a Problem in the Economic War, 1932–38' in *Irish Historical Studies*, vol. XXII, no. 86, pp. 154–5. See also David Harkness, 'Economic War Ends: Ports Returned', in *Irish Times*, 2 January 1969.
23. *Belfast Newsletter*, 26 April 1938.
24. *Irish Times*, 13 January 1969.

NOTES TO CHAPTER 5

1. *Irish Independent*, 15 June 1938; *Belfast Newsletter*, 13 and 20 June 1938.
2. *Sunday Despatch*, 23 October 1938.

Notes

See John Bowman, *De Valera and the Ulster question 1917–73* (Oxford, 1982), p. 196; and reference to *The Times*, 10 February 1939.

4. Robert Fisk, *In Time of War: Ireland, Ulster and the Price of Neutrality 1939–45* (London, 1983), p. 74.

5. Lady Craig's Diary, 2 May 1939, PRONI D1415/B/38.

6. See the remarks of J. W. Nixon and Thomas Henderson, *NIHC Debs*, vol. XXII, cols 1318–19, 4 May 1939.

7. *Irish Times*, 13 December 1939 (Mr E. O'Mahoney, Cork).

8. PRONI CAB4/475/15.

9. W. S. Churchill, *HC Debs*, vol. 371, col. 1718 (27 May 1941).

10. *Annual Register 1940*, p. 98.

11. Fisk, *In Time of War*, p. 161.

12. Craigavon telegram to Chamberlain, 27 June 1940, PRO PREM4/53/2/409. See Paul Canning, *British Policy Towards Ireland, 1921–41* (Oxford, 1985), p. 285.

13. Fisk, *In Time of War*, p. 182.

14. Lady Craig's Diary PRONI D1415/B/38, 11 July 1940.

15. From a report by Brigadier Watson, Officer Commanding Belfast Area, submitted through army headquarters to J. M. Andrews, 28 April 1941, PRONI, CAB9CD/217.

16. *Northern Whig*, 21 April 1941. See Brian Barton, *The Blitz: Belfast in the War Years* (Belfast, 1989), p. 138.

17. PRONI, CAB9CD/217.

18. W. S. Churchill, *The Second World War*, vol. 3: *The Grand Alliance* (London, 1950), p. 539.

19. Bowman, *De Valera and the Ulster Question*, p. 248.

20. *The Times*, 28 January 1942.

21. *Irish Times*, 28 September 1948. See also T. Ryle Dwyer, *Irish Neutrality and the United States of America* (Dublin, 1977), pp. 152–3, which shows the anger of the American Minister to Ireland, David Gray, to the MacRory statement. Gray accused the Cardinal of inciting murder against American troops and implying that they had invaded Ireland.

22. *Belfast Newsletter*, 19 March 1942.

23. Churchill statement on the occasion of the appointment of Andrews as a Companion of Honour, 9 May 1943: *Keesing's Contemporary Archives*, 8–15 May 1943, p. 5756.

24. Herbert Morrison, *The Times*, 15 July 1943.

25. Brooke, *NIHC Debs*, vol. XXIX, col. 79 (24 July 1945).

26. Winston Churchill, *The Times*, 14 May and 13 June 1943.

27. Ronan Fanning, *Independent Ireland* (Dublin, 1983), pp. 152–9.

28. J. M. Andrews, *NIHC Debs*, vol. XXX, col. 1985 (8 October 1946).

29. E. De Valera, *Dail Debates*, vol. 97, cols 2116 and 2568–73 (11 and 17 July 1945).
30. J. H. Whyte, *Church and State in Modern Ireland, 1923–1970* (Dublin, 1971), p. 60.
31. Quoted at length in Fanning, *Independent Ireland*, p. 140.
32. J. A. Costello, *Dail Debates*, vol. 113, col. 385 (24 November 48).
33. Brooke, *NIHC Debs*, vol. XXXII, col. 3665-6 (30 November 1948).
34. Quoted by the French Ambassador to the United Kingdom, René Massigli, in a summary of London reaction. See Archives, Ministry of Foreign Affairs, France (hereafter AMFAF) '1944–49, Europe; Irlande', vol. 11, 'Relations bilaterales: Irlande–GB et Irlande du Nord, Feb. 1948–June 1949', pp. 112–15 (8 December 1948).
35. Fanning, *Independent Ireland*, p. 178.
36. 12 and 13 Geo VI cap. 41, the Ireland Act, 1949, Article 1:(2).
37. C. Attlee, *HC Debs*, vol. 464, col. 1858 (11 May 1949).
38. AMFAF, p. 201 (see note 34).
39. Ibid., p. 209.
40. Ibid,. p. 199.
41. Fanning, *Independent Ireland*, p. 180.
42. Garret FitzGerald, 'Steps towards Reconciliation' in *Fortnight*, no. 21, 9 July 1971, p. 21.
43. Fanning, *Independent Ireland*, p. 180.

NOTES TO CHAPTER 6

1. See John Whyte, *Church and State in Modern Ireland, 1923–1970* (Dublin, 1971), chs 7 and 8; and Noel Browne, *Against the Tide* (Dublin, 1986), chs 9–11.
2. See, for example, Kieran Kennedy, Thomas Giblin and Deirdre McHugh, *The Economic Development of Ireland in the Twentieth Century* (London, 1988), pp. 124–5.
3. John E. Sayers, 'The Political Parties and the Social Background', in Thomas Wilson (ed.), *Ulster under Home Rule* (Oxford, 1955), p. 71
4. David Harkness, *Northern Ireland since 1920* (Dublin, 1983), p. 131.
5. *Annual Register, 1951* (London, 1952), p. 78.
6. R. Fanning, *Independent Ireland* (Dublin, 1983), p. 195.
7. Terence O'Neill, *Ulster at the Cross-roads* (London, 1969), p. 173.
8. *The Times*, 12 April 1965, Supplement, p. ii, 'In the Grip of History'.

9. Ibid.
10. Harkness, *Northern Ireland since 1920*, p. 150.
11. O'Neill, *Ulster at the Cross-roads*, p. 173.
12. J. J. Lee, *Ireland 1912–1985* (Cambridge,1989), p. 429.
13. Ibid., p. 461.
14. *Annual Register, 1972*, p. 42.

NOTES TO CHAPTER 7

1. Tom Wilson, *Ulster: Conflict and Consent* (Oxford, 1989), p. 180.
2. Robert Bell, Robert Johnson and Robin Wilson (eds), *Troubled Times: Fortnight Magazine and the Troubles in Northern Ireland 1970–91* (Belfast, 1991), p. 184.
3. Tom Hadden and Kevin Boyle, *The Anglo-Irish Agreement: Commentary, Text and Official Review* (London, 1989), p. 4.
4. *New Ireland Forum Report* (Dublin, 1984), para. 5.4, p. 28.
5. Ibid., para. 5.2 (3), p. 27.
6. *Northern Ireland: Report of an Independent Enquiry* (London, 1984).
7. *What Future for Northern Ireland?* (London, 1985).
8. The Agreement, signed at Hillsborough, seat of the former Governors of Northern Ireland, on 15 November 1985, was published in full in the press on the following day (see, for example, *Belfast Telegraph*, 16 November 1985). It is also reproduced and closely analysed in Hadden and Boyle, *The Anglo-Irish Agreement*.
9. For the proposal to lift the constitutional ban on civil divorce, the voting figures were 935,842 against; 538,279 in favour. The proposal was thus rejected overwhelmingly, despite a government recommendation for its acceptance.
10. *Common Sense* (Belfast, 1987).
11. *An End to Drift* (Belfast, 1987).
12. *Governing with Consent* (Belfast, 1988).
13. *Belfast Newsletter*, 12 April 1990.
14. *Fortnight*, no. 291 (January 1991), p. 21.
15. Ibid., no. 295 (May 1991), p. 22.

NOTES TO CHAPTER 8

1. *Ireland in Europe: a Shared Challenge*, Stationery Office (Dublin, 1992), pp. 9–10.
2. Ibid.

3. See, for example, J. J. Lee, *Ireland 1912–85: Politics and Society* (Cambridge, 1990); Jonathan Bardon, *A History of Ulster* (Belfast, 1992).

4. Lee, *Ireland 1912–85*, pp. 462–3; and White Paper, *The Accession of Ireland to the European Communities* (Dublin, January 1972).

5. Lee, *Ireland 1912–85*, pp. 489; but see also *New Ireland Forum: a Comparative Description of the Economic Structure and Situation, North and South* (Dublin, 1983); *Understanding and Co-operation in Ireland*, Papers 1–8 and Report 9, published by Co-operation North (Belfast and Dublin, 1980–3); *Irish Statistical Abstracts* (Dublin, annually); and *Northern Ireland, Annual Abstracts of Statistics* (Belfast).

6. Lee, *Ireland 1912–85*, p. 474.

7. Ibid., p. 501.

8. See Garret FitzGerald, *All in a Life* (Dublin and London, 1991), where this phrase appropriately forms part of the title of chapter 14.

9. Lee, *Ireland 1912–85* , pp. 478–9.

10. As note 5.

11. Bardon, *A History of Ulster*, p. 782.

12. FitzGerald, *All in a Life*, p. 90.

13. Ibid., p. 496.

14. Ibid., ch. 16.

15. Ibid., p. 392.

16. Ibid., p. 269.

17. Terence Brown, *Ireland: a Social and Cultural History* (Glasgow, 1981), pp. 135–6

18. The IRA announced a 'complete cessation of military operations' on Wednesday, 31 August 1994.

19. Garret FitzGerald, 'Generosity Needed to bring Island Together', in *Irish Times*, 1 October 1994, p. 10.

INDEX

Abdication crisis, 59
Act of Union, 1
Advisory Committee (NI), 106
Alliance Party, 98, 101, 103, 108,
    112–13
American troops to Ireland, 71
An End to Drift, 111
Andrews, J. M., 48, 67, 71–3, 77–8
Anglo-Irish Agreements (1938), 61,
    64
Anglo-Irish Agreement (1985),
    108–12, 114, 121–2
Anglo-Irish Encounter, 106
Anglo-Irish Financial Settlement
    (1926), 55
Anglo-Irish Free Trade Agreement
    (1965), 91
Anglo-Irish Ministerial Council,
    106
Annual Register, 68, 88, 89
Anti-Partition League, 77
area, 1
Articles 2 and 3 (Irish
    Constitution), 113–14, 124
Articles of Agreement for a Treaty
    (the 'Treaty'), 40–5, 49, 56, 59,
    61, 63
Asquith, H. H., 9–11, 14, 20–3,
    29–30, 131
Atkins, Humphrey, 105, 108
Attlee, Clement, 76, 81, 82

Baldwin, Stanley, 43, 56
Balfour, Arthur, 11
Bates, R. Dawson, 52

Belfast, 2–3, 17, 58–9, 67, 70–1, 93,
    96, 115–16
Belfast blitz, 67, 70, 74
Belfast Newsletter, 50, 58, 60–1, 63–4,
    72
Belfast Telegraph, 28, 87
Beveridge, William, 73, 76, 84
Blaney, Neil, 97
'Bloody Sunday' (1972), 99
Boer War, 4
Borden, Robert, 44
Border Poll, 103
Boundary Agreement (1925), 45–7,
    50
Boundary Commission, 40–5
Brooke, Basil (Viscount
    Brookeborough, 1952), 55–6,
    66, 73, 75–6, 78, 80–1, 86, 91–2
Brooke, Peter, 112–14
Brown, Terence, 125
Browne, Noel, 84–6
Bruton, John, 113
Buckingham Palace Conference, 20
Buckmaster, Lord, 44

Callaghan, James, 105
Campbell-Bannerman, Henry, 8–9
Carlisle Bridge, 48, 51
Carson, Edward, 19–23, 29–32, 42
Casement, Roger, 28
Cavan East by-election, 32
Ceannt, Eamon, 25
censorship, 49, 74, 92
census, 1 (1901), 13 (1911), 84
    (1951), 85 (1961)

centenary, of 1798 Rebellion, 4
Chamberlain, Neville, 62, 66–9
Chichester-Clark, James, 95–6
Churchill, Winston, 42, 67–9, 71,
 73, 75–6
Citizen Army, 25–6
Clann na Poblachta, 79, 85
Clarke, Tom, 12, 25
Colley, George, 119
Collins, Gerry, 113
Collins, Michael, 31, 39, 41–3
Common Agricultural Policy, 120
Common Sense, 110
Community Relations Council
 (CRC), 122–3
Compulsory Military Training Bill
 (1939), 66
Connolly, James, 25
conscription (First World War), 25,
 31–2; (Second World War),
 65–8, 71
Conservative Party, 6–7, 9–11, 14,
 16, 20–1, 23, 34, 39, 44, 102,
 105
*Constitutional Proposals for Northern
 Ireland*, 103
Convention, Irish, 9, 30–1
Cooke, Henry 3
Co-operation North, 123
Cork Film Festival, 116
Corrymeela, 123
Cosgrave, Liam, 103–5
Cosgrave W. T., 43, 45–6, 48–9, 53,
 56, 71, 78
Costello, John A., 79–80, 84–5, 88
Council of Ireland, 35, 45, 103–4
Craig, James (Viscount Cragavon,
 1927), 20, 37, 39–44, 46, 48,
 52–3, 56, 58–9, 62, 64, 66–70
Craig, Lady, 66
Craig, William, 95, 98
Craig–Collins pact, 42
Cranborne, Lord, 71
Cultural Heritage, 122
Cumann na mBan, 25
Cumann na nGaedheal, 49
Currie, Austin, 98

Dail Eireann, 34, 38, 49, 52, 60, 62,
 64
Davis, Thomas, 5, 13, 15

Democratic Unionist Party (DUP),
 98, 101, 105, 111, 123
de Valera, Eamon, 31(1917), 38–9
 (1921), 42–3(1922),
 48–9(1926–7), 52–4(1932–3),
 56–62(1933–7),
 64–9(1938–40), 70–3(1940–4),
 77–8, 81(1948), 88, 90(1957)
Derry Citizens' Action Committee,
 95
Derry Folk Drama and Arts
 festivals, 116
Devlin, Joe, 18
Devlin, Paddy, 98
devolution, 8–9, 11, 102–3, 105,
 108–10, 112
Dillon, John, 18, 28, 29, 31, 32
Dillon, James, 78
disestablishment, 3
divorce, 49, 78, 92, 102, 110
dominion status, 38, 40, 76
Donaldson, Lord, 108
Donegal County Council, 51
Donegall, Lord, 65
Donnelly, Eamon, 57
Duffin, Adam, 29
Dulanty, J. W., 68–9
Dungannon Clubs, 13

Easter Rising, 26–9, 31, 92
*Economic Development in Northern
 Ireland*, 93
Economic Development, 90, 91
Economic war, 53, 55, 57, 59, 61–2
Education Acts (Britain, 1944;
 Northern Ireland, 1947), 86
Education for Mutual
 Understanding (EMU), 122
Edward VII, 8, 10
Eire, 60, 68, 74–5, 79, 82
Electoral law (1934), 57
Emmet, Robert, 12
Enniskillen bomb, 111
Erne Drainage Development Acts
 (NI and Republic), 88
Eucharistic Congress (1932), 56, 58
European Convention on the
 Suppression of Terrorism
 (1977), 111
European Economic Community
 (EEC), 90–1, 103, 117–23

European Monetary System (EMS), 118
Evening Standard, 64
extradition, 102, 109, 111

Falkland Islands, 52
Fanning, Ronan, 82-3
Faulkner, Brian, 96, 99, 103–4, 124
Feetham, Richard, 44
Fermanagh Times, 28
Fethard-on-Sea, 90–1
Fianna, 25
Fianna Fail, 49, 52–5, 57, 61–2, 64, 79, 84–5, 101, 105–6, 119
Fine Gael, 101, 105, 120, 124
Fisher, J. R., 44
Fitt, Gerry, 98, 103, 104, 106
FitzGerald, Garret, 82, 101, 105–7, 109, 120–1, 124–6
Foster, Roy, 26
Foyle Fisheries, 48, 50, 88–9
French, Lord, 1, 32, 125
Friends of Ireland, 76

Gaelic Athletic Association (GAA), 4, 115, 116
Gaelic League, 5, 24
Galloon Island, 54
GATT, 90
General Elections
    British, 6 (1900); 10, 11, 14 (1910); 32, 34–5 (1918); 44 (1924); 76 (1945); 104 (1974)
    Irish, 38 (1921); 43 (1922); 49 (1927); 52 (1932); 53–4 (1933); 59, 61 (1937); 61, 64 (1938); 79 (1948); 85 (1951)
    Northern Irish, 57–8 (1933); 62 (1938); 75 (1945); 81 (1949); 88 (1959); 95 (1969)
George II, 61
George V, 10, 38
George VI, 60
gerrymandering, 50
Gladstone, W. E., 14
Gormley, Joe, 98
Governing with Consent, 112
Government of Ireland Act (1920), 12, 18, 34, 36, 45, 67, 120

Governor-General, 54
Great Northern Railway, 48, 89
Greenwood, Hamar, 32
Griffith, Arthur, 5, **7–8**, 13, 25, 39, 41, 43

Hand, Geoffrey, 44
Haughey, Charles, 97, 101, 106, 112, 120
Health Act (1947), 84
Heath, Edward, 103, 104
Hewitt, John, 115
Hillery, Patrick, 97
Hitler, Adolf, 66
Hobson, Bulmer, 12–13, 26
Home Rule Act (1914), 21, 34
Home Rule Bill (1912), 6, 10–11, 16–19, 34
Home Rule Bills, (1886, 1893), 3
Hume, John, 98, 105, 107
hunger strikes, 106
Hurd, Douglas, 109

Institute of Directors, 112
integrated education, 122
Intergovernmental Conference, 110
Intergovernmental Council, 106
Intergovernmental Meeting, 114
inter-parliamentary body, 106
Inter-Party Government, 79, 85
IRA, 52, 58, 65, 68, **87–9(1956–62)**, 96–7, 103, 106, 111, 115, 126
IRB, 7, 12, 24–5, 31
Ireland Bill, 81
Irish Congress of Trade Unions (ICTU), 92
Irish Constitution (1937), 12, **59–62**, 73, 78, 91–2, 107, 113–14, 124
Irish Council Bill, 9
Irish Division (16th), 22
Irish Free State, 40–3, 45–6, 48, 51–7, 59–61, 80, 117
Irish Independent, 59
Irish Parliamentary Party, 3, 5, 6, 8, 11, 14–16, 28, **30–3**, 35
Irish Society, the, 50–1, 88
Irish Times, 63
Irish Volunteers, 21–2, 24–6, 31
Irish White Paper on accession, 119

joint sovereignty, 102, 107

King, Tom, 109
Kitchener, Lord, 22

Labour Party,
  British: 10, 23, 38, 43, 76–7, 86,
    102, 104–5
  Irish, 25, 52, 120
Lagan College, 122
land annuity, 54–5
Lansdowne, Lord, 30
Lee, J. J., 37, 119
Lemass, Sean, 55, 90–3
Liberal, Party, 3, 6, 8–11, 14, 23, 38,
    132
List, Frederick, 8
Lloyd George, David, 9, 23, 29–30,
    32, 34–5, 38–40, 43
local government, 3, 87, 98
Londonderry, Lord, 51, 53,
Long, Walter, 34–5
Lynch, Diarmuid, 31
Lynch, Jack, 92, 94–7, 105–6

MacBride, John, 25
MacBride, Sean, 79, 81
MacDermott, Sean, 12, 25
MacDonagh, Thomas, 25
MacDonald, Malcolm, 69
MacDonald, Ramsay, 43–4
MacNeill, Eoin, 24, 26, 43, 45
MacRory, Cardinal, 56, 66, 72
Magee University College, 93
Major, John, 113
Mallon, Seamus, 110
Mason, Roy, 105
Massigli, Ambassador, 82
Maxwell, General, 28
McCartan, Patrick, 12
McConnell, Bertie, 98
McCorkell, Senator, 55
McCullough, Dennis, 12–13
McCusker, Harold, 111
McGarry, Sean, 25, 31
McNeill, Ronald, 29
McQuaid, Archbishop, 84
Metcalf, Percy, 48
Military Council (IRB), 25
Military Service Bill (1918), 32
Millar, Frank, 111

Mitterrand, President, 125
Molyneaux, James, 105, 111
Morning Post, 45
Morrison, Herbert, 67–8, 73, 82
Mother and Child Scheme, 84

Naboth, 54
Napier, Oliver, 98
National Convention, 9
National Council, 8
National Democratic Party, 97
National Insurance Acts (GB, 1948;
    NI, 1946), 86
National University of Ireland, 9
Nationalist Party (NI), 97
Ne Temere Decree, 18
New Ireland Forum, 107, 121
New University of Ulster, 93
New York Times, 64
Nordic Council, 108
Northern Ireland Civil Rights
    Association (NICRA), 94–5
Northern Ireland Assembly, 8,
    103–4, 108–10
Northern Ireland Convention, 105
Northern Ireland Economic
    Council, 92
Northern Ireland Executive, 103–4
Northern Ireland Labour Party, 98
Northern Ireland Secretariat, 106
Northern Whig, 44, 54

O'Brien, Conor Cruise, 121
O'Brien, William, 25
O'Connell, Daniel, 2
O'Fiach, Cardinal Thomas, 105
O'Grady, James, 52
O'Hegarty, P. S., 12
O'Higgins, Kevin, 49
O'Kelly, Sean T., 25, 55
O'Neill, Phelim, 98
O'Neill, Terence, 91–5, 98
O'Rahilly, The, 26
O'Regan, Brendan, 123
Orange Order, 51–2, 56, 58
Orr, David, 106
Ostrorog, Minister, 82
Ottawa Conference (1932), 55

Paisley, Ian, 94, 98, 105, 111
Parliament Act, 11

Parliament Bill, 10–11
Parnell, Charles Stewart 3, 5
Pearl Harbor, 71
Pearse, Patrick, 25–6
Peoples' Democracy, 95
Pitt, William, 19
Plunkett, Horace, 25
Political Research Group, 110
Pollock, Hugh, 55, 56
population, 1, 13–14, 16, 36, 52, 57, 84–5, 118, 132
Powell, Enoch, 105
power-sharing, 104
Prior, James, 108–9
Privy Council, Judicial Committee of, 44, 49, 51, 54
Programmes for Economic Development, 90–1
Progressive Unionist Party, 62
Proportional Representation, 50
Protestant and Catholic Encounter (PACE), 123
Protestant Unionist Party, 98
Provisional Government, 26 (1916), 41 (1922)
Public Safety Act (IFS,1931), 52
Pym, Francis, 104

Queen's University, Belfast, 9, 58, 95, 115

Redmond, John, **3**, 5–6, 8–9, 13–16, 18–24 (1914), 28–30 (1916–18), 38, 66
Rees, Merlyn, 105
Republican Labour Party, 97
Republic of Ireland (1949), 76, 79–81
Robinson, Mary, 113
Robinson, Peter, 111
rolling devolution, 108
RTE, 90

Salisbury, Lord, 18
Sayers, John E., 87
sectarian riots, 58
Single European Act (1987), 122
Sinn Fein, 5, 8, 13, 23, 25, 28, **31–5(1918)**, 37–8, 40, 49, 88, 96, 101, 108, 132

Social Democratic and Labour Party, 97–8, 101–11, 113–14, 123
Somme, battle of, 30
South Africa, 7, 15
Special Powers (NI) Act (1922), 52, 94
Spring, Dick, 120
Stephen, Ninian, 114
Stewart, W. J., 62
Stormont, suspension of, 96, 99
Sunday Despatch, 65
Sunday Independent, 59, 84
Sunningdale, 103–4
Suspensory Act (1914), 21

'talks about talks', 112
Task Force, 111
Thatcher, Margaret, 102, 105–6, 108–9, 113, 121
Thomas, J. H. (Jimmy), 5, 13, 15, 25, 54
Times, The, 21, 42, 63–4, 93
Tone, Wolfe, 5
Towards a New Ireland, 106
Troops, to Northern Ireland (1969), 96

Ulster Covenant, 16–17, 36
Ulster Day (28 September 1912), 16, 18
Ulster Defence Association, 110
Ulster Division (36th), 22
Ulster Folk and Transport Museum, 115
Ulster Museum, 115
Ulster Special Constabulary, 51, 67, 94
Ulster Unionist Council, 4, 29, 36, 104
Ulster Unionist Party, 20, 23, 33, 35, 37, 101(Official Unionist Party: OUP), 103, 105, 113, 123
Ulster Vanguard Party, 98
Ulster Volunteer Force, 20, 22
Ulster Workers' Council (1974), 104, 124
Unemployment Insurance Agreement (1935), 63
Unionist Party of Northern Ireland (UPNI), 104

United Irishman, 7
United Nations, 90, 97

Vatican Council (1962–5), 90

Whitaker, T. K., 107
Whitelaw, William, 100, 102, 104
Whyte, John, 78
Wickham, Charles, 68

Wilson, Harold, 104–5
Wilson, Tom, 93
Women Together group, 123
World Bank, 90
Workers Party, 113
Wyndham Land Act (1903), 7, 9

Yugoslavia *v* Irish Republic football
    match (1955), 89